When God Walked Among the Nations

When God Walked Among the Nations

The Leaders and Lessons of the First Great Awakening

Michael F. Gleason

RESOURCE *Publications* • Eugene, Oregon

WHEN GOD WALKED AMONG THE NATIONS
The Leaders and Lessons of the First Great Awakening

Copyright © 2019 Michael F. Gleason. All rights reserved. Except for brief quotations in critical publications or reviews, no part of this book may be reproduced in any manner without prior written permission from the publisher. Write: Permissions, Wipf and Stock Publishers, 199 W. 8th Ave., Suite 3, Eugene, OR 97401.

Resource Publications
An Imprint of Wipf and Stock Publishers
199 W. 8th Ave., Suite 3
Eugene, OR 97401

www.wipfandstock.com

PAPERBACK ISBN: 978-1-5326-8267-4
HARDCOVER ISBN: 978-1-5326-8268-1
EBOOK ISBN: 978-1-5326-8269-8

The Holy Bible, English Standard Version® (ESV®) Copyright © 2001 by Crossway, a publishing ministry of Good News Publishers. All rights reserved.

Manufactured in the U.S.A.

Now to him who is able to do far more abundantly than all we ask or think, according to the power that is at work within us, to him be glory in the church and in Christ Jesus throughout all generations, forever and ever! Amen.

—Ephesians 3:20–21 (ESV)

You are the God who works wonders; you have made known your might among the peoples.

—Psalm 77:14 (ESV)

Soli Deo Gloria!

Contents

Acknowledgements | ix
Introduction: First Things | xi

Chapter 1: Dawn Deferred | 1
Chapter 2: First Lights | 15
Chapter 3: Sunrise in Europe! | 26
Chapter 4: Sunrise in America! | 36
Chapter 5: England Ablaze! | 47
Chapter 6: Cultivating the Harvest | 58
Chapter 7: Lessons | 67

Appendix 1: Sermons by George Whitefield and John Wesley | 75
    a) *The Method of Grace* by George Whitefield
    b) *The Way to the Kingdom* by John Wesley

Appendix 2: Additional Great Awakening Sermons | 101
    a) *The Gospel Method of Salvation; or, The Condemned State of Man by Sin, and the Way Appointed of God for His Recovery Through the Righteousness of Jesus Christ Received by Faith* by Samuel Blair
    b) *An Exhortation to Walk in Christ* by William Tennent

Appendix 3: Society Rules and Orders | 133
    a) *Orders and Expectations for Society Members*
    b) *The Nature, Design, and General Rules of the United Societies*

Bibliography | 139

Acknowledgements

For the interest and support of family and friends, the timely assistance of Dr. D. Elaine Bednar, the permission granted by The Rev. Richard Owen Roberts and Joshua Press, the gracious endorsements from esteemed colleagues, and the editorial insights from Matthew Wimer and the fine staff at Wipf and Stock, I will remain forever grateful.

Introduction

First Things

IN YOUR FERVENT SEASONS of prayer, what is it that you seek above all things? What longing is deeper than the salvation of a loved one, the alleviation of a physical distress, or the mending of a broken heart? What should be counted as the foremost desire of the Christian church, of its godly clergy and laity? Would not the greatest desire, the infinite longing, the highest of all sacred human yearnings be found in the following exhortation of the Apostle Paul?

> He is the image of the invisible God, the firstborn of all creation. For by him all things were created, in heaven and on earth, visible and invisible, whether thrones or dominions or rulers or authorities—all things were created through him and for him. And he is before all things, and in him all things hold together. And he is the head of the body, the church. He is the beginning, the firstborn from the dead, *that in everything he might be preeminent* (Col 1:15–18 ESV, emphasis mine).

Clearly, this text informs us that the supreme hope of godly men and women should be the right and due restitution of all created things to their Maker, and the visible restoration of the preeminence of Christ within both the church and culture. For *he alone* is the image of the invisible God, the creator, the head, the Son—our Lord Jesus Christ! Thus, it is altogether honorable and worthy to study topics related to seasons of genuine historic revival, for during such times our dear and sacred Savior, in all his perfection, is more purely worshiped, more supremely glorified, more wonderfully enjoyed, more deeply known, more reverently loved, and more vigorously obeyed by hearts subdued and concentrated for his service.

INTRODUCTION

Understand me fully, the salvation of a loved one, the alleviation of physical distress, or the mending of a broken heart, if such be your prayers, are honorable requests to share with our gracious Christ. Truly ours is a God, exalted in the supremacy of his being, who does bend low to attend to the whispers of many a broken and lost human soul. Nonetheless I must declare again that highest of all sacred human longings is that the King, in our generation and time, "might be preeminent" within the church, and reign as the undisputed Lord of each human heart! Such was the experience of many who were favored to live throughout the First Great Awakening as the triune God walked among the nations. What a glorious season in the life of the church you are about to discover! I am certain that all but the most distant soul will be renewed with hope as the lessons and leaders of this great epoch are revealed in the forthcoming pages.

Prior to inviting the reader to invest themselves in the central theme of this book, which is revival, a few important distinctions need to be furnished that I believe will provide a greater understanding of this theme in general, and the related lessons from the First Great Awakening in particular. This initial goal will be accomplished by providing a helpful differentiation between *revival* and *renewal*. I will likewise outline the difference between a *word-centered* and an *experience-centered* revival movement. My own perspectives and definitions are primarily developed through careful historical research combined with practical experience in various fields of Christian ministry, having served in ordained ministry for over four decades as well as written in previous publications about each of these respective terms. As we now examine the first set of terms, allow me to propose the following distinction between *revival* and *renewal*:

INTRODUCTION

Revival	Renewal
What God does, commonly through human vessels and always according to the decrees of Scripture, to effortlessly cause personal and corporate reformation resulting in profound conviction, abundant conversions, enlivened obedience to Christ and his word, Spirit-inspired prayer, and glorious worship.	What Christians labor to do, by the power of the Holy Spirit and in submission to the decrees of Scripture, to progress in personal and corporate reformation through disciplined obedience to Christ and his word, Spirit-dependent prayer, genuine worship, heartfelt repentance, and personal evangelism.
Revival is characterized within much of the book of Acts, as illustrated in the following passage: "Now when they heard this they were cut to the heart, and said to Peter and the rest of the apostles, 'Brothers, what shall we do?'. . . So those who received his word were baptized, and there were added that day about three thousand souls" (Acts 2:37, 41 ESV).	Renewal is characterized within many of the commands found in the Epistles, as illustrated in the following words of the Apostle Paul: "work out your own salvation with fear and trembling, for it is God who works in you, both to will and to work for his good pleasure (Phil 2:12b–13 ESV).
Revival acknowledges the *manifest* presence of God, indisputable and piercing within human lives.	Renewal acknowledges the *essential* and *cultivated* presence of God; sometimes quietly present, other times actively present.
Revival is experienced when God is mightily *walking among the nations*, among a church, or within the life of an individual Christian.	Renewal is experienced by an individual Christian, church, or nation who is *walking toward God*.
Word-centered revival produces— • Extraordinary Spirit-prompted prayer. • Profound conviction of sin accompanied by brokenness and genuine repentance, leading to a life marked by holiness. • Scores divinely called to missions and ministry. • Notable social and moral transformation. • Numerous, authentic, and powerful conversions. • Doctrinal, penetrating, and protracted biblical teaching and preaching.	Renewal encourages— • Disciplined Spirit-dependent prayer. • Cultivating a deeper devotion to Christ through spiritual disciplines that foster personal holiness. • A calling to missions and ministry. • An emphasis on social and moral transformation. • The practice of personal evangelism. • Protracted Scripture study accompanied by doctrinally sound teaching and preaching.

INTRODUCTION

Peruse again each respective column and note how the descriptions of every term are contrasted with the summary immediately adjacent. Revival, by means of illustration, is depicted as *what God does,* whereas renewal has its basic origins in *what Christians labor to do.* In revival the ability of the omnipotent God to accomplish whatever he decrees is, by comparison, *effortless.* Contrastingly, renewal is characterized as the *labor* of both the corporate church and the individual Christian. Seasons of word-centered revival, as the discerning reader will soon witness, bear the recurrent fruit of *extraordinary Spirit-prompted prayer, profound conviction of sin accompanied by genuine repentance, notable social and moral transformation, lives marked by personal holiness,* as well as *numerous and powerful conversions.*

Revival, in its essence, is the manifest presence of the holy God *walking* mightily among a people, producing both *indisputable and piercing* transformation in the wake of his path. Renewal, in its essence, is the church or individual Christian *laboring by the power of the Holy Spirit, and in submission to the decrees of Scripture,* to *cultivate a deeper devotion* to the holy God; discovering throughout the process that he is *sometimes quietly present, other times actively present.* Clergy promoting renewal, for example, will entreat the holy God through *disciplined and Spirit-dependent prayer* to produce the fruits of genuine conviction and earnest repentance within their flock, but after months of devoted intercession and doctrinal preaching they may observe the active and convicting work of God evidenced in only a handful of lives. And yet with prayerful and expectant hearts, carried along by the authority of the word and the power of the Spirit, they press on! Pastors advocating biblical renewal will give an appropriate emphasis to social and moral transformation, but after a season of doctrinally rich scriptural teaching may observer only a determined indifference within their members. They are, however, convinced that the *essential presence* of the holy God is in their midst as they gather, even if his visible activity is quiet for a season; and so, with faithful and obedient hearts, depending on the strength that God alone supplies, they press on! Evangelism is likewise practiced within the renewed church, with the evidence of God's sovereign, active, and gracious work apparent in perhaps only a few precious souls who are soundly converted to Christ. This indeed is glorious, but just a fraction of the vast multitudes that discover the new birth throughout the seasons of revival fervor. And yet with grateful, hopeful, and obedient hearts, looking to the One who alone has the power to save, pastors and parishioners alike press on!

INTRODUCTION

The fruit of genuine renewal is evident when the individual Christian or corporate community of faith is joined in a singular "yes," resolving to both study and obey the whole counsel of God as revealed in the pages of sacred Scripture. Renewal is likewise the means through which various historic revivals cultivated their harvest. In a concluding chapter of this book two styles of groups (*society* and *class*) utilized by God to advance the renewal initiated by the First Great Awakening will be examined in detail. It is my hope that much of the material in this particular section will assist the reader in deepening their understanding and practice of renewal principles within their unique contexts of ministry.

The *lessons* of revival are likewise important to master so, if by the gracious mercy of God, the reader experiences a season of genuine spiritual awakening they will be better equipped to cultivate its fruits. And if by God's providence we find ourselves living in a dark season of history, longing for God to walk again among the nations, these lessons will also serve as a reminder of the biblical directives associated with individual and corporate renewal that are applicable *for every day and age*. Four concise lessons are provided in chapter 7, with other related lessons scattered throughout the book. The reader is urged to prayerfully consider how God might desire to apply each lesson to their life and ministry.

Now I invite you to observe another important distinction between *word centered* and *experience-centered* revival movements. My understanding of these terms was notably shaped by the writings of veteran revival scholar, Rev. Richard Owen Roberts. I will share a few of his thoughts related to this theme in the following text:

> As a generalization, revivals fall into two distinct categories: experience-centered and word-centered. Experience-centered revivals, of which the Welsh revival of 1904–1905 and the Jesus people revival of 1971–1972[1] are good examples, tend to last briefly, end abruptly, and result in only minor reforms, if any. Word-centered revivals may be expected to endure a long time, possibly even an entire generation, to restore to the church certain great biblical truths that have been neglected and are almost guaranteed to produce long-range moral and social improvements. Both the sixteenth-century Protestant Reformation and the eighteenth-century Evangelical Revival/Great Awakening are primary examples of this second kind of revival. Confession, prayer, and praise are

---

1. I would also suggest that the minor collegiate visitation in the spring of 1995 would be characterized as an experience-centered revival.

xv

INTRODUCTION

the prominent activities in an experience-centered revival. Spirit-anointed preaching producing profound conviction, glorious resuscitation of individuals and churches, and radical conversions are the expected norm of the word-centered revival.[2]

As before, I will provide a chart[3] to help clarify the important characteristics of each term as they were thoughtfully articulated by Rev. Roberts.

Word-centered Revivals	Experience-centered Revivals
In-depth Spirit-anointed doctrinal teaching is the focus of group meetings, which frequently produces intense conviction, brokenness, confession, genuine repentance, prayer, and praise. Such teaching is aimed at the restoration of great biblical doctrines and practices that have been long neglected: • The majestic attributes of God, Christ, and the Holy Spirit. • Justification by faith alone. • The characteristics of genuine repentance and holy living. • Spiritual disciplines. • Practicing the faith through service, evangelism, and missions.	Testimonies, conviction, confession, prayer, and praise are common occurrences in group meetings. Teaching at such gatherings often lacks depth and substance.
Conversions are both numerous and predominantly authentic.	Numerous conversions are regularly reported, a number of which later prove to be spurious.
Seeking God and his glory is foundational in word-centered movements. In these revivals the preached word of God *moves* throughout a gathering with freedom and extraordinary power.	*Seeking revival experiences* is routinely the focus of participants in experience-centered movements. A number who gather may therefore be *moved* by fleeting emotions, rather than by the Spirit or the word.

---

2. Roberts, *Whitefield in Print*, xii.

3. This chart and related commentary are adapted, with kind permission from the publisher, from the author's book: Gleason, *When God Walked on Campus: A Brief History of Evangelical Awakenings at American Colleges and Universities*, 18–19.

INTRODUCTION

| Word-centered movements endure a long time, restore the church to certain great biblical truths, and produce long-range moral and social improvements. The Protestant Reformation and the First and Second Great Awakenings are superb examples of word-centered revivals. | Experience-centered movements last briefly, end abruptly, and are comparatively devoid of long-term reformation. Such was the case with the 1857–1858 prayer revival, the Welsh revival of 1904–1905, and the Jesus people revival of 1970–1972. |

Compare and contrast again the various descriptions with the adjacent summary. Whereas *seeking God and his glory* is foundational within the word-centered movements, *seeking revival experiences* is often the focus of experience-centered gatherings. Profound, protracted, doctrinal in-depth biblical teaching is dominant within word-centered movements, as is illustrated throughout the various Great Awakening sermons catalogued within appendix one and two. The reader is encouraged to survey these treasured documents, and observe how scripturally soaked and God honoring they are. Examine each thoroughly, and beseech the revival Spirit to enable you to both know and teach the sacred word with a corresponding conviction!

On the other hand, as the experience-centered movements are studied one becomes aware that the leaders routinely provide messages that are comparatively deficient in both depth and substance. Indeed, it can be accurately stated that word-centered revivals produce not only the conviction, confession, prayer, and praise common to experience-centered movements, but also increased occurrences of genuine repentance, authentic conversions, and long-term reformation of both doctrine and practice. The First Great Awakening is an excellent illustration of a word-centered revival, and therefore worthy of ardent study. My research, however, has led me to sadly conclude that the majority of spiritual awakenings, particularly those within the past century, have been experience-centered and thus brief in scope and comparatively deficient in producing the brokenness, spiritual transformation, and lasting purification common to word-centered movements. It is likewise my current concern that the general superficiality of our prevailing Christian culture may well prompt the believing community to look no further than for another short-lived blessing, when the average church and respective community is in deep need of nothing short of sustained biblical, moral, and social reformation!

Does the reader wonder if a titanic revival, a revival so vast in scope that it produces sustained biblical, moral, and social reformation throughout every corner of our deeply troubled nation is even possible in *our* time?

INTRODUCTION

Sometimes, I must admit, my hope languishes as well. It is at these moments that I refresh my spirit with stories, great stories, of how our God walked among the nations in times past; bending, breaking, convicting, converting, renewing, and reviving cultures and people who were hopelessly lost. Do *you* wonder if a revival of this magnitude is possible within *our* decadent era? Then it is time to turn the page, not to a brighter, but to a more horrific age, as you begin your journey into a dark season of history that precedes the glorious event best known as the First Great Awakening.

1

Dawn Deferred

WHAT ERA OF HISTORY do you believe The Rev. Dr. Increase Mather was describing when he stated:

> ... conversions are become rare in this age of the world. ... In the last age, in the days of our fathers, in other parts of the world, scarce a sermon preached but some evidently converted, and sometimes hundreds in a sermon. Which of us can say we have seen the like? ... The body of the rising generation is a poor, perishing, unconverted, and (except the Lord pour down his Spirit) undone generation. Many that are profane, drunkards, swearers, lascivious [obscene], scoffers at the power of godliness, despisers of those that are good, disobedient. Others that are only civil, and outwardly conformed to good order, by reason of their education, but never knew what the new birth means.[1]

The era to which Dr. Mather was referring was the late seventeenth-century—1678 to be exact. From his perspective all was hopeless unless "the Lord pour down his Spirit" and powerfully walked among the nations. Some may suggest that *hopeless* is too strong a term to describe the prevailing state of faith and culture within both Europe and America throughout the decades that preceded the First Great Awakening. Perhaps, however, the following brief analysis of the conditions within the English and surrounding European societies may lead the discerning reader to a similar conclusion.

Faith

The Puritan movement began, and was notably strengthened, during the sixteenth-century as the biblical Reformation spread throughout the believing

---

1. Gillies, *Historical Collections of Accounts of Revival*, 279–280.

community. However, early in the seventeenth-century weeds began to grow among the wheat as throughout Europe Satan's folly became evident. An illustration of this point can be seen as early as 1624 when the philosophy known as Deism found its way into contemporary culture. Although many of the early Deists diverged less radically from orthodox Christianity, the evolution of this philosophy, according to one historian, produced "a religion of reason which ruled out miracles, prayer, and the deity of Christ."[2] The Frenchman best known as Voltaire was perhaps one of the most influential Deist in his day, as well as an outspoken enemy of orthodox Christianity. The rationalistic philosophy that he and others of a similar mind espoused was presented so persuasively that soon many among general populace of England were caught in the grip of this delusion.

While the development of Deistic thought was gradually eroding the Christian worldview, a straightforward attack upon the Puritanical faith was launched in 1662 through an edict known as the Act of Uniformity. Simply stated, the Act of Uniformity was an unscrupulous revision of the Common Book of Prayer that promoted alterations favoring the advancement of state concerns. Furthermore, the clauses of this Act demanded each clergyman to "declare his unfeigned assent and consent to the use of all things in the said book."[3] The 2000 rectors, a fifth of the entire body of clergy at that time, who unconditionally refused to comply with the Act were at once dismissed from their parishes without compensation. Tragically, among the exiled "were the most learned and the most active of their order"[4] including the famous Puritan Richard Baxter, as well as the great-grandfather and grandfather of the eminent eighteenth-century evangelist, John Wesley.

A further hindrance to the advancement of the gospel was the Church of England's official position regarding baptism. Briefly stated, the Church affirmed salvation was the lasting possession of all baptized infants. Many who grew to adulthood under the influence of this erroneous doctrine gained the mistaken notion that by this singular act they possess a "secure admission into heaven,"[5] and therefore could live as they pleased without fear of damnation. Additionally, all English clergymen were obligated to offer Lord's Supper to any person who furnished proof of infant baptism. One can only imagine

2. Cairns, *An Endless Line of Splendor*, 55.
3. Bready, *England: Before and After Wesley*, 21.
4. Green, *History of the English People*, 3:362.
5. Tracy, *The Great Awakening*, 36.

the typical communion table of that day overflowed with participants whose souls had never known the spiritual cleansing symbolized by the bread and wine that were freely consumed in blind ignorance.

The spiritual void created by the expulsion of pious clergy and erosion of sound doctrine was further widened by the traditional practice of clergy selection. For centuries clergy who served the Church of England were customarily nominated by the king, the bishop of the diocese (if funding was secured from outside sources), or by the person or persons who had privately donated the finances required to support their local parish. Thus, it was common to have pulpits filled *not* with the godliest candidate available, but with the associates of kings, bishops, or wealthy townspeople. In fact, when reviewing applicants some would scarcely consider conversion to the Christian faith as a relevant requirement for ministry! One could sorrowfully conclude that many who replaced the courageous two thousand evicted from their pulpits by refusing to comply with the Act of Uniformity were likely to have been greater friends of the state, than friends of the Savior.

It would be inaccurate to suggest that *all* the devoted shepherds had been banished from the land. There was a remnant of clergy throughout this season of decline who, as the next chapter will readily attest, "did their best, according to their lights, to carry out their duties faithfully."[6] At times their labors were even graced by a stirring of the Spirit that produced a taste of the divine fruit commonly reserved, in its fullness, for seasons of genuine and prolonged revival. A review of early eighteenth-century church history indicates that such clergy, and subsequent stirrings of the Spirit, were nonetheless comparatively scarce. On the other hand, the number of clerics who considered the parish as little more than a source of income, rather than a sphere of ministry, was abundant. In fact, "scores of villages never saw their rector, unless perhaps he came to settle some dispute about the tithe."[7]

In this light whole churches, severely neglected by their spiritual leaders, were left to ruin. When touring his province, the Bishop of Carlisle chronicled the following observations as he visited three "active" parishes—"The room is miserably shattered and broken, not one pane of glass in any of the windows. No flooring. No seats. No reading desk." Of another, "The inside of the church was full of water." And of yet another, "The church

---

6. Moorman, *A History of the Church in England*, 287.
7. Balleine, *A History of the Evangelical Party*, 11.

looked more like a pig-sty than the house of God."[8] One parish was so pronounced in its corruption that reports described "person's playing cards on the communion table, drinking and smoking!"[9]

A majority of the Irish clergy, like many from England, were "sons of the gentry, and accustomed to their sporting, drinking, and riotous habits. They had no preparation for ministerial duties but a college degree, and no education, either literary or moral, which had not been obtained among wild young men at college."[10] One cleric, when rebuked by his bishop for drunkenness, piously defended himself by asserting that "he was never drunk on duty."[11] It is no wonder that the pulpits filled by such men were emptied of divine doctrine and power! Distorted by Deistic views, many ministers regarded the Bible as simply "a book, and often a despised book; while Jesus Christ, far from being acclaimed as the incarnate revelation of God and Savior of men, was reduced to the level of a mere ethical teacher—and a misleading one."[12] Yet another historian suggested "the vast majority of sermons were miserable moral essays, utterly devoid of anything calculated to awaken, convert, sanctify, or save souls."[13]

In Scotland, "the old style of preaching" was likewise being laid aside in preference to the exposition of "cold formal addresses."[14] Given the appalling state of the clerical office during this general era, it should come as no surprise that when addressing a group of clergymen Lord Bolingbroke vehemently declared, "the greatest miracle in the world is the subsistence of Christianity and its continued preservation as a religion, when the preaching of it is committed to the care of such un-Christian men as you."[15]

State

With the church in such decline, one might conclude a citizen in this era would look to the state with hopeful expectation that the governing authorities would restore justice and order to the rapidly decaying culture. Indeed

8. Balleine, *A History of the Evangelical Party*, 13.
9. Poole-Connor, *Evangelism in England*, 141.
10. Macfarlan, *The Revivals of the Eighteenth Century, Particularly at Cambuslang*, 11.
11. Cairns, *An Endless Line of Splendor*, 54.
12. Bready, *England, Before and After Wesley*, 40–41.
13. Fish, *Handbook of Revivals*, 45.
14. Macfarlan, *The Revivals of the Eighteenth Century, Particularly at Cambuslang*, 9.
15. Bready, *England, Before and After Wesley*, 91.

the governing authorities of this day *were* busy in service, but it was not the concerns of general populace that were foremost on their agendas, but rather their own fraudulent interest; and their leader, Sir Robert Walpole, set the pace. As an individual, Walpole "was given to drunkenness and gluttony; he lived in open adultery; and having a positive taste for obscenity."[16] As a politician, and England's first prime minister, he believed "that government must be carried on by corruption or by force, and he deliberately made the former the basis of his rule."[17] Illustrations of his personal political ideology are numerous. For example, when surveying members of Parliament Walpole suggested that "all these men have their price." And he was indeed correct, as history records the fact that a 1739 victory in the House of Commons was secured in Walpole's favor only because 234 of the 262 who voted in support were likewise recipients of his financial patronage.[18]

What lifestyle choices were found among a majority of the governing assembly? On various occasions it was noted that Parliament adjourned early because "the honorable Members were too drunk to continue the business of State."[19] Similar to Walpole, both the King and Prince of Wales were also living in open adultery.[20] So acceptable was the practice of infidelity that Lord Chesterfield is said to have written his son a patriarchal letter containing explicit instruction in the "art of seduction."[21] Members of the governing assemblies, in keeping with their leaders, were likewise frequent, public, and shameless in their exercise of marital unfaithfulness.

The moral corruption in church and government spread like a cancer throughout the general populace. Illustrations of this tragic fact are abundant. By means of illustration, nineteenth-century historian Dr. T. Smollett provides the following vista of Britain in 1730:

> England was at this period infested with robbers, assassins, and incendiaries, the natural consequences of degeneracy, corruptions, and the want of police in the interior government of the kingdom. . . . Thieves and robbers were now become more desperate and savage than ever they had appeared since mankind were civilized. In the exercise of their rapine they wounded,

16. Bready, *England, Before and After Wesley*, 120.
17. Lecky, *A History of England in the Eighteenth Century*, 1:426.
18. Bready, *England, Before and After Wesley*, 120.
19. Bready, *England, Before and After Wesley*, 147.
20. Balleine, *A History of the Evangelical Party*, 9.
21. Green, *Short History of the English People*, 736.

maimed, and even murdered the unhappy suffers, through a wantonness of barbarity.[22]

The government's answer to rising lawlessness, according to Samuel Johnson who lived through most of this turbulent time, was to make common and reoccurring violations punishable by death. The rationale, he suggests, was the belief that "one thief on the gallows would terrify other thieves back into honest ways."[23] Thus the government logged 253 *capital offenses* on the Statute-Book, including such trivial crimes as damaging the Westminster Bridge, cutting down a young tree, shooting a rabbit, and stealing property worth five shillings.[24]

Charles Wesley's journal records a time during this general era when he preached to fifty-two felons, each waiting to be hung, including a tender child of ten! When the fated day of execution arrived, all of London was present, "Fashionable people paid for seats on the grand stand . . . and thousands who could not afford seats sucked oranges round the gallows, watching the contortions of the poor wretches as they slowly choked to death, for no drop was allowed, and it took a man a good half-hour to die."[25] Despite this brutal punishment of the condemned, the public hangings "seemed to have no effect in checking the spread of crime."[26]

Those imprisoned endured conditions that were virtually as hopeless as the prisoners whose day at the gallows had already passed. The incarcerated, for example, had no legal claim to food. In 1729 Marshalesa prison, which generally housed seven to eight hundred criminals, reported "upwards of 350 literally dying of starvation."[27] One decade earlier the same institution buried 300 in less than three months! A look inside a typical cell indicates that those not claimed by starvation commonly fell prey to disease and despair. The Castle prison was ". . . horribly overcrowded and disgustingly dirty; men and women, debtors and felons were crowded together all day; at night the women were driven to a dungeon without either windows or beds, to sleep on filthy straw . . . No attempt was made to preserve discipline of any kind."[28] Disease in such conditions spread rapidly,

---

22. Smollett, *The History of England*, 1:580–581.
23. Turberville, *Johnson's England*, 314.
24. Fitchett, *Wesley and His Century, A Study in Spiritual Forces*, 292.
25. Balleine, *A History of the Evangelical Party*, 10.
26. Balleine, *A History of the Evangelical Party*, 10.
27. George, *London Life in the Eighteenth Century*, 307.
28. Balleine, *A History of the Evangelical Party*, 4.

with jail fever, or typhus, small pox, and other pestilence routinely destroying prisoners "in great number."²⁹

Family

Now conceivably after laboring through the preceding accounts surveying the collapse of church, state, and society, the reader might be hesitant to inquire about the general condition of the eighteenth-century family. The hesitation is merited, for when the wickedness of this harsh time covered the continent the traditional family also fell under its shadow, and conceivably no vice was more widely used to erode the once pious homes than alcohol. Indeed, so broad was its influence that in the first decades of this century the death rate, widely attributed to alcohol related causes, surpassed the rate of birth!³⁰ The great influx of liquors during this era is customarily linked to a dispute with France over brandy trade. In retaliation the English governors decided to lift all restrictions for the production and sale of British gin. In a few weeks, "six thousand gin shops were opened in London and Westminster," enticing the wayward soul with advertisements such as, "drunk for 1d, dead drunk for 2d."³¹ By 1725, one of the largest English districts boasted a liquor retailer flourishing at every fifth house!³² Alcohol sales were likewise common at work. The famous Benjamin Franklin, who in 1725 was employed in a London printing house, records that an alehouse boy freely roamed the work floor throughout the day supplying the needs of thirsty workers.³³

The obvious impact of such abuse on the family is readily documented. For instance, many factories distributed weekly wages late Saturday night in public drinking dens. This customary practice caused many a husband and father to return home early Sunday morning "drunk and empty-handed," having only "words and blows" to offer their families.³⁴ Even among men of means, it was the custom to spend "evenings at some public-house or tavern" with the "better class of customer" enjoying the stolen fruits of

---

29. Turberville, *Johnson's England*, 318.
30. Trevelyan, *Illustrated English Social History*, 3:49.
31. Balleine, *A History of the Evangelical Party*, 8.
32. George, *London Life in the Eighteenth Century*, 32.
33. George, *London Life in the Eighteenth Century*, 290–291.
34. Bready, *England, Before and After Wesley*, 148.

seduction in the adjoining parlor.³⁵ The neglected wives likewise sought, among other vices, distilled liquors to fill their emptiness. Some, so daily consumed, provided their children, infants and youngsters alike with a constant supply of spirits. Others, ignoring their little ones altogether, left them "starved and naked at home."³⁶ The tendency of drunken husbands toward the insufferable physical abuse of their children was frequently adopted by their spouses. One horrible story provides a graphic illustration:

> There is the case of Judith Dufour who fetched her two-year old child from the workhouse, where it had just been 'new-clothed' for the afternoon. She strangled it and left it in a ditch in the Bethnal green in order to sell its clothes. The money (one and four pence) was spent on gin and was divided with a woman, who (she said) instigated the crime.³⁷

The dear child in the previous illustration was certainly not alone. A document titled the *London Bills of Mortality* certifies that approximately seventy-five percent of children of all classes born in this period died before their fifth birthday. Those sent to the workhouse or abandoned at infancy to the care of the parish had a survival rate averaging only one in ten.³⁸ The ones who survived beyond five knew different heartaches. A majority of the children above this tender age in the Taunton clothing region and valleys of West Riding, by means of illustration, could *not* be found playing in soft green grass of the meadows, but rather hard at work in the clothing industry earning their daily bread.³⁹ In terms of education, it was not until the advent of the Sunday school movement that any provision, with the exception of the woefully inadequate charity schools, was made for the free and substantive instruction of the poor. In place of school, the common lot of the needy was to be indentured from an early age as an apprentice. While in theory an apprenticeship appeared to be a move upward, in practice it was often a sentence of slow death. A journalist in the early seventeen hundreds provides this commentary:

> "A most unhappy practice prevails in most places," said a writer on the Poor Laws in 1738, "to apprentice poor children, no matter

---

35. George, *London Life in the Eighteenth Century*, 273.
36. George, *London Life in the Eighteenth Century*, 34.
37. George, *London Life in the Eighteenth Century*, 42.
38. Bready, *England, Before and After Wesley*, 142–145.
39. Trevelyan, *Illustrated English Social History*, 3:29.

to what master . . . The master may be a tiger in cruelty, he may beat, abuse, strip naked, starve, or do what he will to the poor innocent lad, few people take much notice, and the officers who put him out the least of anybody . . . it is the fate of many a poor child, not only to be half-starved and sometimes bred up in no trade, but to be forced to thieve and steal for his master, and so is brought up for the gallows."[40]

In the midst of such perversity, the concept of a traditional Christian marriage was likewise swiftly fading. Even at their delicate beginnings, most weddings were stained by the mixture of drink and depravity that typified the culture. Marriages ceremonies, for instance, were frequently conducted in the morning "to ensure the sober senses of the contracting parties." Many such services were known to have been officiated in the pub by "vagabond parsons,"[41] one of whom is credited with conducting 173 in a single day![42] So eroded was the sanctity of marriage that a later prime minister of England, although united to a wife, thought nothing of attending a public performance with his mistress.[43] Similarity, village baptismal records validate the fact that the spread of immorality was nothing short of rampant.[44] This was truly a dark age for the family, a time when "purity and fidelity to the marriage vow were sneered out of fashion."[45]

Moral Bankruptcy

The tragic demise of church, state, society, and family was further advanced by the ready availability of all that was morally perverse. The sensual appetite found more than enough to gratify its cravings through gambling, contemporary drama, literature, or, if one was so inclined, the brothel. By means of illustration eighteenth-century fiction writer, Oliver Goldsmith, describes in the following narrative a few impressions of a London visitor, all of which are quite historically credible:

> Every evening as I return home from my usual solitary excursions, I am met by several of those well-disposed daughters

---

40. George, *London Life in the Eighteenth Century*, 227.
41. Bready, *England, Before and After Wesley*, 147.
42. Lecky, *A History of England in the Eighteenth Century*, 1:117.
43. Green, *History of the English People*, 3:736.
44. Balleine, *A History of the Evangelical Party*, 9.
45. Green, *History of the English People*, 3:736.

of hospitality, at different times and indifferent streets, richly dressed, and with minds not less noble than their appearance . . . One takes me under the arm, and in a manner forces me along; another catches me round the neck, and desires to partake in this office of hospitality; while a third kinder still, invites me to refresh my spirits with wine.[46]

Indeed, the "taste for the pornographic was avid, if not insatiable," attracting even noted clergy of the day to sample its poison fruit.[47] One brave clergyman firmly resisted by taking a bold stand against the vulgarity of his age through the publication of a work that analyzed contemporary theater. With great care he evaluated 7000 "instances" from the plays performed in his present era, documenting no less than 1,400 texts from the Bible that had been gravely offended within their collective scripts![48] Despite the noble efforts of a few, "The stage seemed to exist for nothing but to preach and propagate vice, and almost all literature of the time was stamped with the mark of the Beast."[49]

Gambling likewise flourished among noblemen, fashionable ladies, and common laborers who squandered their respective earnings with shameless abandonment. Profits from the English lottery, for example, were so immense that the Westminster Bridge was built chiefly from its revenue.[50] In many local villages, the brutalization of innocent animals was added to the exchange of gambled earnings as cockfighting grew in popularity. Each participant would furnish their best bird, which would fight to the death—winner takes all. According to Johnson, "all classes indulged in it . . . county fought county, town fought town, village fought village; peer and gentlemen fought among themselves."[51] Dogs, bears, bulls, badgers, and other species of foul were also utilized in similar contests to satisfy the swelling cultural passion for loathsome torture and lurid gain.

Conceivably the greatest illustration of the moral bankruptcy evident within eighteenth-century Europe was the vile plundering, capture, and subsequent vending of fellow human beings. Initiated by the Treaty of Utrecht in 1713, Great Britain agreed to annually furnish 4800 slaves of

---

46. Goldsmith, *Citizen of the World*, 27.
47. Bready, *England, Before and After Wesley*, 163.
48. Lecky, *A History of England in the Eighteenth Century*, 1:190.
49. Balleine, *A History of the Evangelical Party*, 9.
50. Lecky, *A History of England in the Eighteenth Century*, 1:157.
51. Turberville, *Johnson's England*, 372.

African descent to South America for a period of 30 years.[52] A contract they fulfilled, and again renewed in 1748; but at what cost to the native? One historian suggests that the total number of slaves transported from Africa most probably "runs into millions, while the processes of tribal warfare, capture, transportation, suicide, acclimatization and early 'discipline' account for the death of perhaps equal numbers."[53] Indeed, "Both numerous and malignant were the economic and political corruptions which, during most of the eighteenth-century, attacked the social life of Britain and her expanding empire; but most devastating of them all, by far, was the slave traffic."[54]

Dawn Deferred in America

Now perchance in leaving the despair of eighteenth-century Europe the reader, in their journey to America, may hope that within this new land the flame of the Puritan faith was still brightly burning. But alas, although there was indeed a fire in this nation, its origins were not from above. We look to a prominent theologian and pastor of this era, Jonathan Edwards, for a description of the prevailing state of society within his town of Northampton, Massachusetts:

> Licentiousness for some years prevailed among the youth of the town; there were many of them very much addicted to night-walking, and frequenting the tavern, and lewd practices, wherein some, by their example, exceedingly corrupted others. It was their manner very frequently to get together, in conventions of both sexes for mirth and jollity, which they called frolics; and they would often spend the greater part of the night in them, without regard to any order in the families they belonged to; and indeed family government did too much fail in the town.[55]

Throughout the remaining pages of this chapter the reader will likely observe that the moral and spiritual corruptions apparent in the small town of Northampton were woefully common, in varying degrees, throughout the entire nation. While it is true that the declension in America was

---

52. Fitchett, *Wesley and His Century, A Study in Spiritual Forces*, 293.
53. Bready, *England, Before and After Wesley*, 102.
54. Bready, *England, Before and After Wesley*, 110.
55. Edwards, *Jonathan Edwards on Revival*, 9.

"neither so evident nor so disastrous as on the continent of Europe,"[56] the citizens in this new land had similarly become so depraved that nothing short of a sovereign work of the holy God would be adequate to restore piety among the people. The following brief overview of the dominant mood of American faith and culture throughout the decades that preceded the Great Awakening will give ready credence to this charge.

Faith and Culture

One who has seriously pondered the eminent works of our Puritan founders will realize that theirs was a faith where the ardent study of sound biblical doctrine was inseparably joined with earnest and heartfelt obedience. Seventeenth-century church members, for example, who demonstrated little evidence of a genuine conversion experience would likely have been challenged by their Puritan brethren as to the authenticity of their profession; for it was the Founder of their faith who taught that "Not everyone who says to me, 'Lord, Lord,' will enter the kingdom of heaven, but the one who does the will of my Father who is in heaven."[57] In this light it is easily understood how the following words, spoken by a famous cleric who lived during this general era, were an accurate portrayal of the prevailing moral conditions evident in New England approximately *one hundred years prior* to the ministry of Jonathan Edwards—"I have lived in a country seven years, and all that time I never heard one profane oath, and all that time I never did see a man drunk in that land. Where was that country? It was New England!"[58] If such was the common state of early American religion and society, what caused the wretched demise of this once authentic faith throughout the subsequent decades?

The reasons for the breakdown of faith throughout this dismal era were manifold, but undoubtedly one of the greatest influences was the historic Halfway Covenant, established at the Synod of 1662. Briefly stated, this agreement granted church membership to unregenerate persons, baptized in infancy, who demonstrated "understanding [in] the doctrine of faith, and publicly professing their assent thereunto; not scandalous in life, and solemnly owning the covenant before the church wherein they give up themselves

---

56. Wood, *The Inextinguishable Blaze*, 53.
57. Matt 7:21, (ESV).
58. Gillies, *Historical Collections of Accounts of Revival*, 280.

and their children to the Lord, and subject themselves to the government of Christ in the church, their children are to be baptized."[59]

Under the instruction of this doctrine, reasonably civil, baptized, but unconverted adults were denied nothing within the church except participation in Holy Communion, which was still reserved strictly for the converted. Tragically it was Solomon Stoddard, grandfather of Jonathan Edwards, who later led a crusade to eliminate this one last precious distinction and permit unconverted church members to join the regenerate around the Lord's Table. When defending his viewpoint Stoddard wrote, "sanctification is not a necessary qualification to partaking of the Lord's Supper," and "the Lord's Supper is a converting ordinance."[60] This clear rejection of sound biblical doctrine, although vehemently opposed by Increase Mather and numerous others, soon became a common practice throughout much of New England. This procedure become so well established that clergymen who refused the Lord's Supper to baptized unconverted members of a local church could be taken to civil court and duly prosecuted![61] The result, according to one historian, was that within the church at large "the unconverted soon outnumbered the converted."[62]

One can understand how many of the young men raised in such churches, who also decided to enter the ministry, were likewise unconverted. Regrettably, Stoddard frequently also championed his firmly held conviction that the "unconverted ministers have certain official duties which they may lawfully perform."[63] Thus many pulpits were filled with clergy who called the masses to follow a Savior whom they had never known. And what was the fruit of their labor? In New Jersey the common parishioner was known to be "careless and carnal." The distinguished Samuel Blair, who resided in Pennsylvania, lamented the fact that true religion among the churches in his region "was dying and ready to expire its last breath of life." The majority of the churches in Virginia and Maryland were in a similar plight. Samuel Whitman, a native of Connecticut, declared that religion had "degenerated into an empty form" and is "languishing in all parts of the land."[64] Truly, Increase Mather was accurate when he stated:

59. Tracy, *The Great Awakening*, 4.
60. Tracy, *The Great Awakening*, 4.
61. Tracy, *The Great Awakening*, 2.
62. Lescelius, "The Great Awakening" *Reformation and Revival Journal* 4, 3:27.
63. Fish, *Handbook of Revivals*, 49.
64. Wood, *The Inextinguishable Blaze*, 54–55.

> . . . conversions are become rare in this age of the world. . . . In the last age, in the days of our fathers, in other parts of the world, scarce a sermon preached but some evidently converted, and sometimes hundreds in a sermon. Which of us can say we have seen the like? . . . The body of the rising generation is a poor, perishing, unconverted, and (except the Lord pour down his Spirit) undone generation. Many that are profane, drunkards, swearers, lascivious [obscene], scoffers at the power of godliness, despisers of those that are good, disobedient. Others that are only civil, and outwardly conformed to good order, by reason of their education, but never knew what the new birth means.[65]

From his perspective, all was hopeless unless "the Lord pour down his Spirit," and walked again among the nations. But take heart, dear reader, as you turn the chapter to read of our loving Lord who, at first through gentle visits to sporadic villages and towns, and then through a blaze that covered the continents, did indeed "pour down his Spirit," and walked afresh with sovereign rule among the nations.

---

65. Gillies, *Historical Collections of Accounts of Revival*, 279–280.

2

First Lights

As was abundantly illustrated in the previous chapter, there was no hope for spiritual revival within either Europe or America save the merciful intervention of God. Yet even throughout these wretched times God was at work. Quietly and purposefully, he was calling and equipping a remnant of gospel messengers to be the first lights of a spiritual awakening so powerful that its influence would saturate two spiritually dry continents. Observe how our longsuffering King, in the darkest of times, appointed messengers and subsequent seasons of spiritual refreshment so that you might find courage to pray for a similar grace in our day!

The First Lights in Europe

Consider, for example, the work of God in Wales through the life of Griffith Jones, a Welsh shepherd boy called to ministry. A pioneer in itinerant field preaching, his formal ordination to ministry was conferred in 1709. Seven years later he was appointed to the rectory of Llandowror, Wales. Almost immediately did God favor his ministry with uncommon spiritual power, as is verified through portions of the following letters written during this common era:

> When Mr. Jones is invited to preach anywhere, and also when he preaches in his own church, in which there does not belong (as parishioners) save ten or twelve small families, it is to be admired what a numerous congregation he has to administer to, having generally above five or six hundred auditors, nay, sometimes a thousand, a number not to be met within Wales besides, on the like occasion.... By his preaching the drunkards became sober, the Sabbath-breakers are reformed; the prayerless cried for mercy

and forgiveness; and the ignorant were solicitously concerned for an interest in the divine Redeemer.[1]

Jones likewise understood the importance of teaching the awakened masses to read so their instruction in the Scriptures might be further advanced. To satisfy this burden, the Circulating Welsh Charity School was established by Jones in 1730, growing from 37 schools in 1737 to nearly 4,000 at the time of his death (1761).[2]

Among the thousands who, by the grace of God, were powerfully transformed through the preaching of Jones was an unconverted clergyman by the name of Daniel Rowland. Although Rowland was "far more interested in sport than in Christianity,"[3] curiosity led him to attend a service in a nearby village at a time when Jones was the featured evangelist. That very night Rowland was sovereignly converted, returning to his parish in Llangeitho a transformed man! Besides continuing in dutiful service to his chapel, he joined the ranks of the itinerant clergy and preached with increased authority to the multitudes that followed him from one village to another.

Space will only allow the consideration of one additional Welsh revivalist, Howell Harris, whose ministry was similarly used by God to usher the early dawn of the Great Awakening. A schoolmaster by vocation, Harris was soundly converted in 1735 from a life of vile sin. As a result of his new birth he journeyed from house to house boldly confronting the spiritual lethargy that had consumed his district. Through his tenacious labor the Spirit opened many hearts to genuine repentance, as confirmed by the following account furnished by nineteenth-century historian Luke Tyerman, "His congregation increased, and the house in which they met could not contain them. Many of his hearers became penitent, and cried to God for the pardon of their sins. Family worship in numerous instances was begun. The churches were soon crowded, and likewise the Lord's Table."[4] Numbered among those converted was Howell Davis, destined by the call of God to become a renowned Welch pulpiteer, particularly among the churches in Pembrokeshire.

The majority of local clergy however, did not share in the delight of this awakening, but with jealous hearts fervently opposed the methodology

1. Wood, *The Inextinguishable Blaze*, 42.
2. Cairns, *An Endless Line of Splendor*, 57.
3. Wood, *The Inextinguishable Blaze*, 45.
4. Tyerman, *The Life of The Reverend George Whitefield*, 1:168.

of Howell Harris. In a final attempt to discredit his ministry, the governing powers in his village evicted Harris from his teaching post at a local school. Despite increased public censure, the tenacious Harris declared he was commissioned by God and not man, and thus began *full-time* service as an itinerant evangelist! To this end he preached throughout Wales "to crowded congregations thirty or forty times every week,"[5] watching with certain joy the Great Awakening unfold.

Within the neighboring shores and highlands of Scotland, the first lights of revival were likewise evident. William M'Culloch, for example, who faithfully served a small parish in Cambuslang from 1731 until his death in 1771 recorded:

> From almost the very commencement of the century, there were in Scotland indications of returning power. The habitations of horrid cruelty abroad, and the abominations of immorality at home, being both glaring, began to engage the public mind. The country was not so far gone as not to feel, at least in many places, a want of gospel light and gospel warmth in the pulpit.[6]

As the Great Awakening advanced, the esteemed revivalist George Whitefield visited Cambuslang to join forces with M'Culloch for a series of meetings. Although written in 1742 after the actual genesis of the Awakening, the reader will certainly be encouraged by the evident work of God demonstrated in the following report penned by Whitefield's hand:

> At mid-day I came to Cambuslang, and preached at two to a vast body of people; again at six and again at nine at night. Such commotions, surely, were never heard of, especially at eleven o'clock at night. For an hour and a half there was much weeping, and so many falling into such deep distress, expressed in various ways, as cannot be described. . . . Mr. M'Culloch preached, after I had done, till past one in the morning; and then could not persuade the people to depart. In the fields all night might be heard the voices of prayer and praise.[7]

A clergyman by the name of Walter Ross, who served a perish in Kilmour Easter, likewise noted "unusual visitations at the communion seasons . . . when people would travel as far as fifty miles to share the blessing."[8]

---

5. Tyerman, *The Life of The Reverend George Whitefield*, 1:169.
6. Macfarlan, *The Revivals of the Eighteenth Century, Particularly at Cambuslang*, 31.
7. Tyerman, *The Life of The Reverend George Whitefield*, 2:5–6.
8. Wood, *The Inextinguishable Blaze*, 117.

Another contemporary of the time, writing again of the early awakenings in Scotland, reported the believers in various parts of the country witnessed "shining evidences of divine power and presence, with ministers and people."[9] As the following chronicle will attest, the effects of such experiences were frequently visible within the church, community, and family:

> After the public worship is over, there are meetings in all parts, where neighboring families join in prayer, reading, and repetitions of sermons, . . . Ordinances are very punctually attended on Lord's days; and diets of catechizing in whatever part of the parish they are kept on week-day, are much crowded by people from other parts. The civil magistrate has had no crimes here . . . for many years; . . . And . . . the people are very diligent and industrious in their secular callings.[10]

Our gaze now moves from Scotland to Germany, where the great movement known as Pietism was born. Pietism began in the late seventeenth-century as a renewal effort among the German Lutheran Churches, with Philip Jacob Spener and August Herman Francke serving as its primary catalysts. Spener's approach, implemented first within his parish in Frankfurt/Main, was to invite Christians to gather in small groups to discuss sermons and study Scripture. A radical idea in his day! Later, he proposed the following six-point plan whose bold ideals must have stood in stark contrast to the listless and superficial Christianity prominent throughout the church in his century—"(1) more intensive Bible study, (2) more lay activity, (3) Christianity to be practiced in daily life, (4) no coercion in religious matters, (5) a reform of theological training, and (6) more edifying preaching instead of rhetoric and dogma."[11] His writing called for a drastic revision of church life, and was met with approval by many in Germany. These first lights of response within the believing community were a merciful sign that the Son of light was withdrawing the darkness that had, for so long, covered the land.

A more intense leader, August Herman Francke, implemented similar disciplines that resulted in his expulsion from a university in Leipzig and subsequent dismissal from a pastorate in Erfurt. Seemingly undaunted by opposition, by God's grace and the assistance of Spener, he secured an appointment at the new University in Halle in 1692. Possessing boundless

---

9. Gillies, *Historical Collections of Accounts of Revival*, 454.
10. Gillies, *Historical Collections of Accounts of Revival*, 454.
11. Durnbaugh, *European Origins of the Brethren*, 33.

zeal and strong organizational abilities, God enabled Francke to transform Halle into the center of world-wide Pietist activity. The fruits of his labor led to the establishment of an orphanage, hospital, schools, seminary, missionary associations, and Bible societies. Various denominations and missionary efforts that flourished throughout the Awakening trace their origins to this gracious work of the Spirit.

Early in the eighteenth-century, a devout young man by the name of Christian David was likewise seeking a place of refuge in Germany for a small persecuted community of believers known as the Unity of the Brethren. During his pilgrimage, the God of history masterfully guided David to a well-known Count of the day, Nicholas Ludwig von Zinzendorf, who had been influenced by Pietist ideals and subsequently established a society of devout believers on his Moravia estate. When, on behalf of his community, Christian David approached Zinzendorf with a request to settle on his land, the response of the Count was both joyful and immediate, "Let as many as will of your friends come hither; I will give them land to build on, and Christ will give them the rest."[12] Over the next years other dispersed believers joined this Moravian community known as Herrnhut, which initially gathered as an independent society who shared an early affiliation with the Lutheran Church.

On August 12, 1727, in a joint communion service at a Lutheran Perish in Berthelsdorf, the Holy Spirit visited the Moravian congregants assembled for worship with a veritable Pentecost. One writer records, "The fire of the Lord fell and they were lost in wonder, love and praise. They left the house of God 'hardly knowing whether they belonged to earth or had already gone to heaven.'"[13] This spiritual baptism gave rise to protracted prayer, persistent piety, and unparalleled missionary zeal. In fact, the reader will soon discover that the outward piety of the Moravian believers had a profound impact on none other than John Wesley prior to his conversion. Starting in 1732, those called from Herrnhut to foreign missionary service traveled to the Caribbean, Greenland, and throughout the American colonies. One historian suggests God had empowered their obedient efforts to such an extent that "the most successful Protestant missions of the whole colonial period were undoubtedly those conducted by the Moravians."[14]

---

12. Lewis, *Zinzendorf: The Ecumenical Pioneer*, 45.
13. Wood, *The Inextinguishable Blaze*, 69.
14. Sweet, *The Story of Religion in America*, 237.

The First Lights in America

As was the case in Europe, the footprints of God were likewise visible throughout America decades before the actual genesis of the Great Awakening. One such outpouring, although sadly brief in duration, was prompted by a communal response to an apparent judgment of God upon New England. The event, and subsequent revival, is described below by historian Gillies:

> In 1679, the Massachusetts government called a Synod of all the churches in that colony to consider and answer these two most important questions. 1. What were the evils that have provoked the Lord to bring his judgements on New England? 2. What is to be done so that these evils may be reformed? And among their answers to the second question, the Synod advised the several churches to an express and solemn renewal of covenant with God and one another, with which many complied, and thereupon there was a considerable revival of religion among them . . . And many thousand spectators will testify that they never saw the special presence of the great God our Savior more notably discovered than in the solemnity of these opportunities.[15]

One assembly that was also visited by seasons of spiritual blessing during this general era was the flock of Solomon Stoddard, grandfather to Jonathan Edwards. Although not consumed with the protracted fire of revival until the arrival of his grandson, the historic Congregational Church at Northampton was favored with no less than five *harvests*, as Stoddard called them, throughout his tenure.[16]

The turn of the century likewise found measures of grace poured out on city of Truntnon, close to the great metropolis of Boston, through the ministry of a clergyman by the name of Samuel Danforth. In a letter where he describes the awakening, Danforth states "religion flourishes to amazement and astonishment."[17] Three hundred renewed souls were the outcome of this particular divine visitation! Further south, the Windham Connecticut parish of Samuel Whiting witnessed the hand of God draw eighty *new* members into the church, all within a period of six months. This was understood by many to be an unprecedented work of the Spirit, considering the total population of his small town was a mere two hundred families.

---

15. Gillies, *Historical Collections of Accounts of Revival*, 281.
16. Lescelius, "The Great Awakening" *Reformation and Revival Journal* 4, 3:30.
17. Wood, *The Inextinguishable Blaze*, 57.

What delight must have been experienced among the pious in Windham as they observed the newly converted inhabitants of their community filled with "love, joy, thanksgiving and praise."[18]

On his way down the Atlantic seaboard the Spirit of God was initiation a powerful work among the people in the New Jersey Raritan valley through the ministry of a Dutch Reformed pastor named Theodore Frelinghuysen. Frelinghuysen had been serving among the Dutch speaking people since the winter of 1720, and throughout his tenure tenaciously confronted the dead orthodoxy that was wide-spread among the Dutch Reformed Churches in American. Simply stated, he preached the necessity of conversion and holy living, while dogmatically proclaiming that both the Eucharist and church membership were to be exclusively offered only to those who were circumcised of heart.

Instead of bending in contrite repentance, his parishioners steadily defied both the man and his message. Finally, in a concluding act of malicious desperation, the church leaders compiled and sent a detailed list of alleged grievances against Frelinghuysen to the denominational officials in Amsterdam. The Spirit of God, however, had determined not to heed the complaints of the unconverted but instead bring a glorious revival to this spiritually cold assembly. Illustrations of the extraordinary awakening in the churches served by this noteworthy man are furnished in the following account recorded by historian Charles Maxson:

> The elders and deacons were converted one after another, until the last deacon made his new confession in 1725. . . . The congregations of the domain increased, and there were numerous conversions among people who were not before upon the roll of the churches. In some years, particularly in 1726, the ingathering was so great proportionately as to give a foregleam of the time when Whitefield should come flaming through the country.[19]

The influence of Frelinghuysen was not, however, simply limited to those parishioners under the authority of his pulpit. By divine providence a spirited clergyman by the name of Gilbert Tennent served a parish in the nearby town of Brunswick, New Jersey, and subsequently befriended Frelinghuysen. Young Tennent had been aptly trained by his father, William Tennent Sr., in the famous Log College located adjacent to his Presbyterian Church in Neshaminy, Pennsylvania. Numerous Great

---

18. Wood, *The Inextinguishable Blaze*, 57–58.
19. Maxson, *The Great Awakening in the Middle Colonies*, 15–16.

Awakening preachers, including Samuel Blair[20] and James Finley, credit their theological roots to this humble academy whose graduates also had a notable impact on Princeton University during its early years. Biblically competent in his own right, Gilbert embraced both the message and methodology of his Dutch mentor, which led to a similar fury from among his parishioners. The fury was widespread, and led to a division among churches and clergy alike; between the *Old Sides*, who counted all baptized church members as regenerate regardless of spiritual fruit or the lack thereof, and the *New Sides*, who preached that conversion with corresponding evidence of regeneration was necessary for all who confessed a genuine faith in the Lord Jesus Christ.

Despite the controversy, Gilbert's New Brunswick church experienced the strong winds of revival. The anointing on his pulpit ministry, both before and throughout the Awakening, is captured in the following commentary by Whitefield—"Never before heard I such a searching sermon. He went to the bottom indeed, and did not daub with untempered mortar. He convinced me, more and more, that we can preach the gospel of Christ no further than we have experienced the power of it in our hearts. I found what a babe and novice I was in the things of God."[21] Gilbert Tennent continued to serve as an itinerate preaching alongside Whitefield from 1739 until the winter of 1741, when he was called to serve the Second Presbyterian Church of Philadelphia.

Another Tennent, by the name of William, joined his brother John who was serving the Presbyterian parish at Freehold as their cleric.[22] This

---

20. Samuel Blair (1712–1751) was born in Ulster, Ireland, and later journeyed to America where he was educated at the legendary Log College in Neshaminy, Pennsylvania. In November of 1733 he was licensed to preach by the Presbytery of Philadelphia, moving in May of 1735 to New Jersey for term of ministerial service in the churches of Middletown and Shrewsbury. In 1740 Blair was called to serve in a Pennsylvania town commonly referred to as Fagg's Manor. Soon after beginning this new work, Blair established a school similar to the Log College where he trained some of the most influential Presbyterian ministers of that century. In that same year, and to the certain joy of Samuel Blair, God graced the congregation of Fagg's Manor with a remarkable revival of religion. A sermon by this admired Great Awakening preacher titled *The Gospel Method of Salvation* is furnished in appendix two.

21. Tracy, *The Great Awakening*, 53.

22. William Tennent (1705–1777) was born in County Antrim, Ireland, and immigrated to America with his family in 1718. Along with his brothers Gilbert, John, and Charles, he was educated at the Log College under the tutelage of his father, William Tennent senior. After recovering from a near fatal illness, he served the Presbyterian Church at Freehold, New Jersey, for the remainder of his natural life. Like Blair, during

congregation had, according to the initial impressions of John, "been given up for their abuse of the gospel." Despite the spiritual corruption evident within the assembly, John witnessed the glorious fruits of spiritual awakening during the first several years of his ministry. The following record furnished by his elder brother William describes this season of grace, "During this short time, his labors were greatly blessed; so that the place of public worship was unusually crowded with people of all ranks; . . . It was no uncommon thing to see persons in the time of hearing, sobbing as if their hearts would break."[23] Following the untimely death of John, William was called in the fall of 1733 to fill the Freehold pulpit, and observed with certain joy that the grace and power of God continued to prevail. Again, the record of William furnishes a glimpse into this most sacred time:

> . . . the blessing of his labors, to the conviction and conversion of souls, was more discernible some months after his death, than at any time in his life; . . . I must further declare, to the honor of God, that he has not yet left us, although awfully provoked by our crying crimes; but ever since that more remarkable outpouring of his Spirit, has continued to bless his own ordinance, to the conviction, conversion, and consolation of precious souls, so that every year, some, more or less, have been in a judgement of charity added (savingly) to his mystical body, to his holy name be all the glory![24]

One final story must still be told, particularly because of its central place in the Awakening. The story surrounds the Northampton Massachusetts Congregational Church where Solomon Stoddard, grandfather to Jonathan Edwards, was serving as the appointed minister. With amazing grace, and despite the numerous and appalling theological errors detailed in chapter one that defined the ministry of Stoddard, God visited the church with no fewer than five reported seasons of spiritual refreshment throughout his administration. In 1727 Jonathan Edwards, son of a clergyman and Yale graduate, arrived in Northampton at the request of his grandfather to assist with pastoral duties. By God's sovereign decree, the providential death of Solomon Stoddard in 1729 opened the door for young Edwards to assume pastoral oversight.

---

various seasons young William's ministry also experienced a gracious outpouring of God's revival Spirit. A sermon by this choice clergyman titled *An Exhortation to Walk in Christ* is furnished in appendix two.

23. Gillies, *Historical Collections of Accounts of Revival*, 285–286.
24. Gillies, *Historical Collections of Accounts of Revival*, 286.

Almost from the beginning, the great reformed doctrines preached by Edwards burned within the souls of the residents of this New England town, causing a profound conviction of sin. By divine providence conviction led to repentance, and repentance was followed by a season of revival that produced its first converts in December of 1734. The following account from Edward's pen furnishing the details of this heaven-sent visitation:

> And then it was, in the latter part of December, that the Spirit of God began extraordinarily to set in, and wonderfully to work amongst us; and there were very suddenly, one after another, five or six persons, who were to all appearances savingly converted, and some of them wrought upon in a very remarkable manner. ... so that in the spring and summer following, *anno* 1735, the town seemed to be full of the presence of God ... Our public assemblies were then beautiful, the congregation was alive in God's service, every one earnestly intent on the public worship, every hearer eager to drink in the words of the minister ... This work seemed to be at its greatest height in this town in the former part of the spring, in March and April. At that time God's work in the conversion of souls was carried on amongst us in so wonderful a manner, that, so far as I can judge, it appears to have been at the rate at least of four persons in a day; or near thirty in a week, take one with another, for five or six weeks together. When God in so remarkable a manner took the work into his own hands, there was as much done in a day or two, as at ordinary times, with all endeavors that men can use, and with such a blessing as we commonly have, is done in a year.[25]

And thus, according to Edward, "Satan seemed to be restrained, till towards the latter end of this wonderful time, when God's Holy Spirit was about to withdraw."[26] What was the fruit of this heavenly encounter within the Northampton Congregational Church? No less than 300 professing conversions![27]

As marvelous as the Northampton revival was for the local congregants, it was also intended by the Creator to be the very spark that soon ignited a purifying fire throughout New England. Nineteenth-century historian Joseph Tracy documents this wonderful story:

---

25. Edwards, *Jonathan Edwards on Revival: A Narrative of Surprising Conversions*, 12–21.
26. Edwards, *Jonathan Edwards on Revival: A Narrative of Surprising Conversions*, 25.
27. Sweet, *The Story of Religion in American*, 189.

FIRST LIGHTS

The report of the state of things at Northampton spread into other towns, where many "seemed not to know what to make of it," many ridiculed it, "and some compared what we called conversion, to certain distempers." Great numbers, however, who came to Northampton and saw for themselves, were differently affected, and not a few of them, from various places, were awakened and apparently brought to repentance. In March, 1735, the revival began to be general in South Hadley, and about the same time in Suffield. It next appeared in Sunderland, Deerfield, and Hatfield; and afterwards at West Springfield, Long Meadow, and Enfield; and then in Hadley Old Town, and in Northfield. In Connecticut, the work commenced in the First Parish in Windsor, about the same time as at Northampton. It was remarkable at East Windsor, and "wonderful" at Coventry. Similar scenes were witnessed at Lebanon, Durham, Stratford, Ripton, New Haven, Guilford, Mansfield, Tolland, Hebran, Bolton, Preston, Groton, and Woodbury.[28]

Yet one additional conversion, unknown to either Jonathan Edwards or the Northampton parish, occurred in the spring of 1735 across the cool grey waters of the Atlantic on the continent of Great Britain. The young convert was an Oxford scholar by the name of George Whitefield, who I believe could not have imagined that three years following the day of his new birth he would be crossing these great waters as a missionary to New England and beyond. Indeed, over the course of the next thirty-five years, Whitefield braved seven individual missionary trips to America. On his second missionary journey he actually visited Northampton, and at the request of Johnathan Edwards delivered a powerful series of messages from the Congregational Church pulpit! And now to the life, calling, and ministry of the one chosen by God to be among the most influential human instruments in augmenting the Great Awakening in both Europe and America, George Whitefield.

---

28. Tracy, *The Great Awakening*, 13.

3

Sunrise in Europe!

EARLY IN THE EIGHTEENTH-CENTURY, the God of history planted a seed of blessing within the dry European soil. That seed was George Whitefield. To those who surrounded the Bell Inn in Gloucester England on December 16, 1714, the birth of young George may have appeared as simply a family blessing. In the eyes of God, however, there was to be a national, indeed an international blessing that was destined to flow from the future life of this infant son; for it was this human vessel, George Whitefield, whom God was pleased to use as one of the primary evangelists to usher in the full light of a revival best known as the First Great Awakening. The home of his parents, Thomas and Elizabeth Whitefield, provided what most would have considered an unusual environment to raise a child destined for such extraordinary spiritual promise. His father, a prosperous wine merchant and innkeeper, was with him for only a few brief years, dying unexpectedly when he was but a tender lad of two. Under the guidance of his widowed mother, who assumed the singular responsibility for parenting seven growing children as well as the primary supervision of the family business, the Inn both endured and prospered.

What was Whitefield's early childhood like? In portions of his *Journal* he confesses with deep remorse to unruly childhood and adolescent behaviors— "I was so brutish as to hate instruction, and used purposely to shun all opportunities of receiving it. . . . Lying, filthy talking, and foolish jesting I was much addicted to, . . . Numbers of Sabbaths have I broken, and generally used to behave myself very irreverently in God's sanctuary."[1] Nonetheless, this same unruly boy also acknowledged that he "was always fond of being a clergyman," and often imitated "the ministers reading prayers."[2] Perhaps

---

1. Whitefield, *George Whitefield's Journals*, 37.
2. Whitefield, *George Whitefield's Journals*, 38.

one could conclude that his childhood was filled with the contrasting pulls common to many a mortal soul. It was in his tenth year that his mother remarried, a union described by Whitefield as "an unhappy match."[3] Under the new but deficient administration of his stepfather the Inn suffered terribly and was nearly lost. As a result young Whitefield, then only fifteen, left his studies at St. Mary de Crypt to work for the next year and a half alongside his family to ensure the survival of their livelihood.

His move away from formal education was only temporary, as through a series of events he was visited at his mother's home by an old classmate who was financing his college education by laboring as a servitor. With the encouragement of his mother, along with the promise of a similar post, Whitefield revitalized his studies and within two years was enrolled as a student at Oxford. Although this season of life found the contrasting lure of good and evil again awakened within his soul, the upward pull of God prevailed drawing him to a pious Oxford group who "lived by rule and method,"[4] known also as the Methodists. It was in this society that young Whitefield first became acquainted with Charles and John Wesley, both of whom were also unconverted and yet equally passionate in their pursuit of holiness. It was likewise through this affiliation that Whitefield received a copy of a book titled *The Life of God in the Soul of Man*. According to his *Journal*, it was through reading this volume that he first grasped the fact that true religion was not simply the practice of pious deeds, but "a union of the soul with God"; a union so powerful that one would literally became "a new creature."[5] Aroused by a new and terrible knowledge that despite his zealous spiritual disciplines he was by no means "a new creature,"[6] Whitefield searched his soul in desperate anguish until the spring of 1735 when, according to his own testimony, "After a long night of desertion and temptation, the Star, which I had seen at a distance before, began to appear again, and the Day Star arose in my heart. Now did the Spirit of God take possession of my soul, and, as I humbly hope, seal me unto the day of redemption."[7]

Thus, with exceeding joy, the soul of George Whitefield was eternally united with God! Over the next year he confirmed a strong and lifelong commitment to the supreme adequacy of the holy Scriptures and, in particular,

3. Whitefield, *George Whitefield's Journals*, 39.
4. Whitefield, *George Whitefield's Journals*, 46.
5. Whitefield, *George Whitefield's Journals*, 47.
6. Whitefield, *George Whitefield's Journals*, 47.
7. Whitefield, *George Whitefield's Journals*, 58.

the doctrines related to the necessity of the new birth and justification by faith alone. Whitefield's subsequent Scripture studies solidified his unyielding devotion to the Bible, as the following *Journal* entry will attest:

> My mind being now more open and enlarged, I began to read the holy Scriptures upon my knees, laying aside all other books, and praying over, if possible, every line and word. This proved meat indeed, and drink indeed, to my soul. I daily received fresh life, light, and power from above.... About this time God was pleased to enlighten my soul, and bring me into the knowledge of his free grace, and the necessity of being justified in his sight by *faith only*. ... Most of us have been taught this doctrine of Christ, and, I hope, shall be willing to die in the defense of it.[8]

Increased spiritual zeal prompted the young convert to engage in works of evangelism, service, and mercy. His sphere of ministry was seemingly as broad as the love God had placed in his heart, and included routine service to various religious societies, the poor, the sick, the destitute, as well as those in prison.

About one year following Whitefield's rebirth Dr. Benson, who resided as the Bishop of Gloucester, invited the promising twenty-one year old to anticipate his blessing "whenever you come for Holy Orders," dismissing his customary practice to not ordain anyone "under three-and twenty."[9] Although Whitefield's *Journal* records how carefully he weighed the spiritual and moral responsibilities of the ministerial office prior to his actual ordination, God soon moved his heart to accept the Holy Orders at Gloucester Cathedral on June 20th, 1736. Thus, the formal ministry of George Whitefield began. Ten days following, the newly ordained minister preached his first official sermon at St. Mary de Crypt, the Church in which he was baptized and had also received early schooling. The reader will delight in the unpretentious wonder experienced by the young evangelist as he recounted his inaugural sermon in the following letter to a friend:

> Curiosity, as you may have easily guessed, drew a large congregation together. The sight at first a little awed me; but I was comforted with a heartfelt sense of the Divine presence, ... As I proceeded, I perceived the fire kindled, till at last, though so young, and amidst a crowd who knew me in my childish days, I trust I was enabled to speak with some degree of gospel authority. A few mocked, but

---

8. Whitefield, *George Whitefield's Journals*, 60, 62.
9. Whitefield, *George Whitefield's Journals*, 67.

most for the present seemed struck; and I have since heard that a complaint has been made to the bishop that I drove fifteen mad. The worthy prelate, as I am informed, wished that the madness might not be forgotten before next Sunday.[10]

Following this humble June morning, George Whitefield preached an estimated eighteen thousand sermons[11] over the course of thirty-four years throughout a titanic revival that consumed two continents.[12] Such a future, I dare say, was probably beyond the imagination of the young cleric as he descended from the pulpit of St. Mary de Crypt on that most eventful Sunday. Read, for example, the following altogether modest aspirations recorded in his *Journal* upon returning to Oxford shortly after his ordination—"In a short time I began to be more than content in my present state of life, had thoughts of abiding at the University, at least for some years, to finish my studies, and do what good I could."[13]

Reasonable ambitions for a lad of 21 years, but the God of revival had different plans. Seemingly unbeknownst to young Whitefield, the sovereign God had appointed him to be among the primary human catalysts through whom the Great Awakening would advance. Consider, by means of illustration, the following reports recorded by Whitefield that began approximately two months following the date of his ordination:

> I preached at Bishopsgate Church, the largeness of which, and the congregation together, at first a little dazed me; but, by adverting to God, and considering in whose Name I was about to speak my mind was calmed, and I was enabled to preach with power. The effect was immediate and visible to all; . . . I also read prayers every evening at Wapping Chapel, and preached at Ludgate Prison every Tuesday. . . . The Chapel was crowded on the Lord's Days.[14]

Throughout the months of profitable ministry in and around the Bishopsgate Church, as well as subsequent service within a small parish inside the town of Dummer, Whitefield was grappling with a written challenge from his friend and comrade John Wesley, requesting he consider ministerial service in America as a missionary to Georgia. His personal wrestling was resolved through a decision to accept the call to missionary service.

10. Tyerman, *The Life of The Reverend George*, 1:50.
11. A sermon by Whitefield titled *The Method of Grace* is furnished in appendix one.
12. Wood, *The Inextinguishable Blaze*, 80.
13. Whitefield, *George Whitefield's Journals*, 76.
14. Whitefield, *George Whitefield's Journals*, 77.

Within several months, both the Bishop in Gloucester and the Archbishop of Canterbury sanctioned his appointment. Immediate plans were made by Whitefield for departure, but God's itinerary for the young evangelists registered a different plan. Providence caused a delay in sea travel for the duration of a full twelve months during which time the detained missionary received more heaven-sent invitations to speak than he was able to fulfill. Dawn was waning in England, and a brilliant sunrise was about to appear over the continent! Be reminded, dear reader, of the wretched condition of the church as documented in chapter one, and contrast those despairing reports with the following excerpts, again from Whitefield's *Journal*, describing an awakening whose morning light was now find its way into even the darkest corners of England:

> (January in Bristol) I preached all the lectures on weekdays, and twice on Sundays besides visiting the Religious Societies. The word, through the mighty power of God, was sharper than a two-edged sword. The doctrine of the new birth and justification by faith in Jesus Christ . . . made its way like lightning into the hearer's consciences. (March in Glouchestershire) Neither church nor house could contain the people that came. I found uncommon manifestations granted me from above. (May to June, again in Bristol) I preached, as usual, about five times a week; but the congregation grew, if possible, larger and larger. It was wonderful to see how the people hung upon the rails of the organ loft, climbing upon the leads of the church, and made the church itself so hot with their breath, that the steam would fall from the pillars like drops of rain. (September, various places) Henceforward, for near three months successively, there was no end of the people flocking to hear the word of God. . . . when I preached, constables were obliged to be placed at the door, to keep the people in order. . . . One might, as it were, walk upon the people's heads; and thousands went away from the largest churches for want of room. They were all attention, and heard like people hearing for eternity.[15]

What pain in parting must have been felt by many revived souls when George Whitefield left his homeland on the sixth of January, 1738, to embark on his first missionary journey to America! This inaugural visit was cut short when he was summoned back to England to secure priest's orders. During this brief four-month excursion, however, he confirmed the need of an orphanage in Georgia, a pursuit that occupied a central place in his ministry

---

15. Whitefield, *George Whitefield's Journals*, 81–89.

throughout the remainder of his life. Although the first lights of awakening were known to many of those whom Whitefield served throughout the brief initial sojourn in and around Georgia, the full sunrise of revival was to be realized during his second missionary journey that began after his arrival in Cape-Lopen, near Philadelphia, in late October of 1739.

What of the intermittent year spent in Europe between the first and second evangelist tour? To answer that question, we will return to the mother continent, the shores of Ireland to be exact, where the exhausted evangelist landed in mid-November of 1738 after several difficult months at sea. As the *Journals* penned by Whitefield after his arrival are reviewed, they reveal that the fires of revival were consuming considerable portions of Europe, as through God's sovereign decree the once fallow fields were now ripe unto harvest.

The reports of spiritual awakening, however, occurred in an environment where there was increasing opposition to Whitefield, particularly from the vindictive clergy who in growing numbers denied him the use of their churches. Their resistance was divinely used to move Whitefield from the closed sanctuary pulpits to the open meadows, where the crowds were magnified in vast proportion. "I thought," said Whitefield while standing upon Hannam Mount, "it might be doing the service of my Creator, who had a mountain for his pulpit and the heavens for his sounding board, and who, when his gospel was refused by the Jews, sent his servants into the highways and hedges."[16] And indeed the Creator was pleased to have his creation utilized for such a purpose, as rich and poor alike gathered by the tens of thousands to hear the gospel presented with great clarity and conviction from the mouth of a young twenty-four year old evangelist. And now observe the sunrise of this Great Awakening throughout seven glorious months documented in the following *Journal* entries:

> (November, 1738 in Ireland) I preached this morning at the Cathedral to a very numerous audience, who seemed universally affected. (December in England) . . . I had an opportunity of preaching in the morning at St. Helen's, and at Islington in the afternoon, to large congregations indeed, with great demonstration of the Spirit, and with power. . . . The old doctrine about justification by faith only, I found much revived. . . . Preached nine times this week, and expounded near eighteen times, with great power and enlargement. I am every moment employed from morning till midnight. There is no end of people coming and sending to me,

16. Tracy, *The Great Awakening*, 48.

and they seem more and more desirous, like newborn babes, to be fed with the sincere milk of the word. (January, 1739) Stayed home on purpose to receive those who wanted to consult me. From seven in the morning till three in the afternoon people came, some telling me what God had done for their souls, and others crying out, "what shall we do to be saved?" . . . Preached twice with great power and clearness in my voice to two thronged congregations, especially in the afternoon, when I believe near a thousand people were in the churchyard, and hundreds more returned home that could not come in. . . . Expounded twice afterwards, where the people pressed most vehemently to hear the word. (February) . . . I preached a sermon on the Penitent Thief to the poor prisoners at Newgate, . . . Many seemed much affected, and I hope the power of the Lord was present to awaken them. . . . I hastened to Kingswood. At a moderate computation, there were about ten thousand people to hear me. The trees and hedges were full. All was hush when I began; . . . and God enabled me to preach for an hour with great power. (March in Wales) At six in the evening, I talked for above an hour and a half, and prayed with the Religious Society, whose room was quite thronged. God was with us of a truth. I think I never spoke with greater freedom and power, and never saw our congregation more melted down. The love of Jesus Christ touched them to the quick; most of them were dissolved into tears. (March in England) I went to a place called the Fishponds, on the other side of Kingswood, where about two thousand were gathered together. . . . having no better place to stand upon, the wall was my pulpit; . . . My preaching in the field may displease some to timorous, bigoted man, but I am thoroughly persuaded pleases God, and why should I fear anything else? . . . I really believe no less than twenty thousand were present at Rose Green. Blessed are the eyes which see the things which we see. Surely God is with us of a truth. To behold such crowds, stand about us in such an awful silence, and to hear the echo of their singing run from one end of them to the other, is very solemn. . . . I visited two Societies, were God was pleased to give us great tokens of his presence, and the way up to the last room was so exceedingly thronged that I was obligated to go up by a ladder through the window. . . . In the evening I expounded again in Weaver's Hall to a most crowded and attentive assembly. People follow more and more; there is a divine attraction in the word of God. Still draw us, O Lord, and we shall still come after thee. (April in Wales) The church (in Comihoy) not being quite large enough to hold half the congregation, I preached from the cross in the churchyard.

The word came with power.... Many thousands were from all parts to hear me, and God gave me such extraordinary assistance, that I was carried out beyond myself. (April in England) I and my friends got safe to Thornberry, where I had appointed to preach on this day, ... The minister, I find, was offended at my doctrine, and therefore would not lend me the pulpit again. However, there being a thousand people waiting to hear the word, I stood upon a table and taught in the street. All was solemn and awful around us; everyone was behaved with gravity, and God gave me freedom of speech.... I hastened to Gloucester and preached in the Booth Hall to, I believe, near five thousand people. Extraordinary power God was pleased to give me. God will work, and who shall hinder? (May) Reached Northampton ... At seven, according to appointment, I preached to about three thousand hearers on a common near the town, from the starting post. I preached with wonderful pleasure, because I thought I had actually possession of one of the Devil's strongholds.... I preached (at Bedford) from the stairs of a windmill ... to about three thousand people; and God was pleased to give me such extraordinary assistance, that I believe a few, if any, were able to resist the power wherewith God enabled me to speak. (June) Preached at nine o'clock in the morning at Thaxted ... to upwards of a thousand people, and with such sweetness and power, as I have not felt since I came into Essex. All around me were melted into tears.... I went in company with many friends to Gloucester, where I preached at seven o'clock in the evening to a large and more affected congregation than ever. Blessed be God, the word has free course. Oh, that it may run and be glorified through all the earth. (July) At seven o'clock in the evening I preached at Baptist Mills to about six or seven thousand people, who were much melted by the power of God's word.... Numbers came from neighboring towns. My congregation was as large again as when I preached here last (Cirencester). God enabled me, weak as I was, to speak boldly. How heavily do I drive when God takes off my chariot wheels, that I may learn to be meek and lowly in my own eyes. Lord, give me humility, or I perish. (August—Departure for his second missionary venture to the America.)[17]

Prior to embarking on a voyage with Whitfield to New England, the perceptive reader might be wondering about the numerical accuracy of the stories that report immense crowds, throughout both Europe and America, who gathered to hear messages of grace from the young evangelist. The

---

17. Whitefield, *George Whitefield's Journals*, 182–317.

skepticism is certainly understandable, particularly considering the spiritually corrupt state of the church and the corresponding moral depravity evident within the general populace.

To address this concern, I would like to invite the reader to join me in Philadelphia at the beginning of Whitfield's second missionary journey, where we discover a generous amount of reporting from secular newspapers furnishing detailed accounts of the Great Awakening. At this time, for example, the renowned Benjamin Franklin was the owner of the *Pennsylvania Gazette,* and under the direction of his editorial management one hundred and sixty-four stories related to the Great Awakening were printed between the years 1739–1748.[18] In fact, "in 1740 alone Franklin printed forty-four items on the revival in the *Gazette,* only three of which were critical of the movement."[19] This statistic is particularly important to note due to the fact that, although Franklin was an acquaintance of Whitfield, he did not share his orthodox doctrinal convictions.[20] In this regard, it could be safety assumed that the reporting within his paper was based upon an objective and unbiases account of these events, rather than a desire to advance any particular religious viewpoint. Furthermore, historian Lisa Smith suggests "the *Gazette's* reporting on the religious events of the 1740s reflects the general trend seen in papers throughout the colonies."[21]

With this historical background in mind, the May 22, 1740 excerpt copied on the following page from the *Pennsylvania Gazette* should prove to be insightful. The general details of this newspaper article appear again in another printed document, the *Journals* of George Whitfield, where the same events are described in comparable terms. The reader will soon observe the reporting in Whitfield's *Journal* of his ministry in cities of Philadelphia, Nottingham, and Fagg's Manor in May 1740, each of which are included in the next chapter, are strikingly similar to the following *Gazette* excerpt. It would be logical to suppose that the newspapers would be eager to correct fallacious stories related to the Great Awakening, particularly those that were simultaneously printed in Whitfield's *Journal.* The fact that numerous stories within the *Journal* of Whitefield are replicated, to a greater or lesser degree, by the secular press only confirms the assumption that what Whitfield recorded in his *Journals* was nothing less than a verifiable account of

---

18. Smith, *The First Great Awakening in Colonial American Newspapers,* 17.
19. Smith, *The First Great Awakening in Colonial American Newspapers,* 19.
20. Smith, *The First Great Awakening in Colonial American Newspapers,* 17.
21. Smith, *The First Great Awakening in Colonial American Newspapers,* 17.

God walking among the nations! Read now the following extract from the May 22, 1740 *Pennsylvania Gazette*, and ready your heart to discover that these wondrous accounts are also reported a hundred-fold in towns, cities, and villages throughout New England and the southern colonies.

> This evening the Reverend Mr. Whitfield went on board his Sloop here, in order to sail for Georgia. On Sunday he preached twice at Philadelphia, and in the evening (he preached his Farewell Sermon) it is supposed he had near 20,000 hearers. . . . The presence of God was much seen in the assemblies, especially at Nottingham and Fogs [Fagg's] Manor, where the people were under such deep soul distress, that by their cries they almost drown'd his voice.[22]

---

22. Smith, *The First Great Awakening in Colonial American Newspapers*, 18.

4

Sunrise in America!

FOLLOWING A YEAR OF virtual glory throughout various portions of Europe, Whitefield again set sail for New England, departing the European shores on the seventeenth of August, 1739. Central in his thoughts was the desire to establish the Georgian orphanage, a dream that found its fulfillment in January of the following year in the town of Savannah, and was likewise sustained with funds raised by Whitefield throughout his tenure. As for the spiritual condition of the land, the reader may recall how God had previously advanced the first lights of revival throughout New England and the southern colonies in the early years of the eighteenth-century, as well as through the recent visit of Whitefield in the summer of 1738. Yet most students of history would agree it was the second missionary journey that had been ordained by God to be "the greatest single evangelistic tour in New England's history and the most remarkable and widespread quickening the American colonies had known."[1] As its influence spread, few could deny that our Lord had commanded the full sunrise of revival previously experienced in parts of Europe to envelop America as well!

Although initially greeted by large crowds upon his arrival in Philadelphia on the eighth of November and New York one week following, those who disdained both the man and his message soon arose in equally increasing number to express their fury. The greatest opposition was again from the clergy who, when disputing the clear biblical doctrines regularly espoused by Whitefield and other evangelical revivalists, furnished the believing public with clear evidence of their covetous core and theological impotence. Similar to Europe, with heartening exceptions here and there, frequently closed pulpits sent the evangelist into the open air, where the glad tidings were published with freedom to the masses.

1. Wood, *The Inextinguishable Blaze*, 62.

The reader would be wise to remember that the wondrous fruit of the Great Awakening in America was not without its price, as brave souls of various denominations stood uncompromised in their proclamation of the gospel despite widespread public hostility. And yet, to quote the captain of this season, "when God will work, who can hinder?"[2] Indeed, the work and pleasure of our sovereign God, in every seasons of history, will be accomplished! The subsequent accounts, again from the *Journal* of Whitefield, will readily attest to this truth.

As was chronicled previously, this particular missionary tour was inaugurated in Philadelphia, where a collective audience of eight thousand persons gathered for two consecutive evenings of exhortation in early November. "Even in London," Whitefield reflectively writes, "I never observed so profound a silence. Before I came, all was hushed exceedingly quiet."[3] Certainly an indication that the holy God was among the masses! Two weeks later, again in Philadelphia, the holy One produced fruit of a different nature as recorded in the following November twenty-sixth *Journal* entry, "The word came with great power, and people now apply to me so fast for advice under convictions, and so continually crowd in around me."[4] The preceding account, in greater or lesser degrees, was to be the norm throughout the coming year where by his own calculation Whitefield preached approximately "one hundred and seventy five times in public, besides exhorting very frequently in private."[5] As with the recounting of the Great Awakening in Europe, we will likewise follow the footsteps of the evangelist in America from November of 1939 throughout 1740, visiting churches, homes, prisons, and countryside where he preached the word with consecrated authority.[6]

> (November, 1739, in Philadelphia) Preached at six in the evening from the courthouse stairs to about six thousand people. I find the number that came on Tuesday to my house greatly increased and multiplied. . . . After preaching my house was filled with people

2. Whitefield, *George Whitefield's Journals*, 350.
3. Whitefield, *George Whitefield's Journals*, 343.
4. Whitefield, *George Whitefield's Journals*, 357.
5. Whitefield, *George Whitefield's Journals*, 499.
6. In the midst of this wondrous awakening, a disheartening event occurring throughout the duration of Whitefield's historic second missionary tour to America involving a division with his friend and colleague, John Wesley, over various doctrinal issues. A synopsis of their controversy, as well as their eventual reconciliation, can be found in the prefatory notes for appendix one.

who came in to join in Psalms and family prayer. My body was weak, but the Lord strengthen me. Many wept most bitterly while I was praying. Their hearts seem to be loaded with a sense of sin, only the preparation for the visitation of Jesus Christ. (New York) Preached in the fields to upwards of two thousand at three in the afternoon; and expounded at six in the evening to a very strong and attentive audience in Mr. Pemberton's meeting house. . . . Preached as usual in the afternoon at the meeting house to a full congregation, and again at night to a great multitude standing around the doors, besides those that were within. (Nashaminy) Set out for Nashaminy . . . where old Mr. Tennent lives, and keeps an academy . . . We came there about twelve, and found above three thousand people gathered together in the meeting house yard, and Mr. William Tennent preaching to them because we were beyond the appointed time. When I came up, he soon stopped and sang a Psalm, and then I began to speak. At first the people seem unaffected, but in the midst of my discourse the hearers began to be melted down and cried much. . . . Lord, remember thy church, and revive thy work among us in the midst of these days. (December at Whiteclay Creek) The weather was rainy, but upwards of ten thousand people were assembled to hear the word. (Bath-Town) Preached at noon to nearly a hundred people, which I found was an extraordinary congregation, there being seldom more than twenty at church. (January, 1740, at Charleston) . . . I preached in the afternoon in one of the Dissenting meeting houses, but was grieved to find so little concern in the congregation. . . . Finding the inhabitants desirous to hear me a second time, I preached at the French church at eleven in the morning, and blessed be God, I saw a glorious alteration in the audience, which was so great that many stood without the door. (January 1740 to March 1740) During these months Whitfield spent a significant amount of time in and around Savannah, Georgia, finalizing plans and beginning construction on the orphan house. (March in Savannah) Nearly forty children are now under my care, and nearly one hundred mouths are daily supplied with food from our store. The expense is great, but our great and good God, I am persuaded, will enable me to defray it. (April in Philadelphia) . . . I preached to upwards of ten thousand people, . . . Hundreds were graciously melted; . . . The word of God every day mightily prevails, and Satan loses ground apace. (Greenwich in the West Jerseys) There being a mistake made in the *News* about the place where I was to preach, I had not above fifteen hundred hearers. (Author's note—who among us would not delight in preaching at such a *mistaken* gathering?) At first, I thought I was speaking to stocks and stones; but before I had done, a gracious melting was visible in most that heard. (New York) Preached this morning from a scaffold erected for that purpose, to a somewhat less congregation than last night, but with much greater power; for toward the conclusion of my discourse, God's Spirit came upon the preacher and the people, so they were melted down exceedingly. (May in Freehold) With them (William and Gilbert Tennent) I set out for Freehold, . . . Oh how sweetly did the time guide on, and our hearts burn within us, when we open the Scriptures and communicated our experiences to each other! (Pennyback) Preached at Pennyback, . . . to about two thousand people, and came back to Philadelphia, about two in the afternoon. Agreed to build my negro schools on the land which I have lately purchased. Preached in the evening, and afterwards began a society of young men, many of whom I trust, will prove to be good soldiers of Jesus Christ. Amen. (Philadelphia) . . . I preached my farewell sermon to very near twenty thousand hearers. . . . I cannot well express how many others, of all sorts, came to give me a last farewell. I never saw a more general awakening in any place. Religion is all the talk; and, I think I can say, the Lord Jesus has gotten himself the victory in many hearts. . . . What I mostly fear is, now that there is a general awakening, the people will not know where to go for proper food, and thereby fall into different sects and parties. Lord Jesus, look upon them, and let not Satan divide them again; but raise them up pastors after thy own heart. Amen and amen. (Nottingham) It surprised me to see such a multitude gathered together, at so short a warning, and in such a desert place. I believe there was near twelve thousand. . . . As I proceeded, the influence increased, till, at last, (both in the morning and the afternoon), thousands cried out, so that they almost drowned my voice. Never did I see a more glorious sight. . . . After I finish my last discourse, I was so pierced, as it were, and overpowered with a sense of God's love that some thought, I believe, I was about to give up the ghost. (Fagg's Manor) Preached at Fagg's Manor, . . . The congregation was about as large as that at Nottingham. As great, if not a greater commotion was in the hearts of the people. Most were drowned to tears. The word was sharper than a two-edged sword. (June in Savannah) . . . when we came to public prayer, the Holy Ghost seem to come into the congregation like a mighty rushing wind, carrying all before it. I had not long begun, before several fell weeping sorely, and the number still increased till young men and maidens, old men and children, were all dissolved into tears and mourning after Jesus. . . . God has often been pleased, since my return to make himself known in our sanctuary and has caused a mighty power to attend to the word preached, both in public and private. Providence seems to smile upon the orphan house, and to prosper everything I take in hand. (July In Charleston) Went to church in the morning and afternoon, and heard the Commissary preach as virulent, unorthodox, and inconsistent a discourse as ever I heard in my life. His heart seemed so full of choler and resentment; and, out of the abundance thereof, he poured forth many bitter words against the Methodists (as he called them) in general, and me in particular, ... (Ashley Ferry) Found myself still weaker, but was strengthened to preach under the tree near Mr. C's meeting-house at ten in the morning, it being now too small to contain the congregation. People seem to come from all parts, and the word came with convincing power.... (Charleston) At my first coming the people of Charleston seemed to be wholly devoted to pleasure.... But now the jewelers and dancing-masters begin to cry out that their craft is in danger.... But the reformation has gone further than externals. Many moral good sorts of men, who before were settled on their lees, have been awakened to seek after Jesus Christ; ... Indeed, the word often came like a hammer and a fire. (August, in Charleston) Being weak in body, I have preached once each day (except on Sundays); ... I scarce know the time wherein I did not see a considerable melting in some part of the congregation, and often it spreads over the whole of it. Several times I was so weak before I began to preach that I thought it almost impossible for me to get through half the discourse; but the Lord quickened, enlightened, and supported me above measure. Out of weakness, I became strong. (September at Newport in Rhode Island) At ten in the morning, and three in the afternoon, according to appointment, I read prayers and preached in the church. It is very commodious, and will contain three thousand people. It was more than filled in the afternoon, persons of all denominations attending. God assisted me much. I observed numbers affected, and had great reason to believe the word of God had been sharper than a two-edged sword in some of the hearers' souls.... In the evening I went privately, as I thought, to a friend's house, but the people were so eager to hear the word that in a short time, I believe, more than a thousand were before the door, besides those that were within, and filled every room of the house. (Roxbury) Preach in the morning at Roxbury to many thousands of people, from a little assent. Several came afterwards to me, telling how they were struck at that time under the word, and a minister wrote to me thus: "... I think I never saw a more attentive audience, or more weeping eyes than yesterday and Monday. The Holy Spirit, the Author alone of all spiritual life, seemed in a very wonderful manner to be moving upon the waters of the sanctuary, breathing upon the dry bones. For my own part I was much affected, and gave our glorious Lord the praise." ... I preached ... in the afternoon, on the common to about fifteen thousand people. Oh, how did the word run! (October in Hampton) Preached in the morning, though not with so much freedom as usual, at Hampton, to some thousands in the open air.... Some, though not many, were affected. God's spirit bloweth when and where it listeth. (Portsmouth) People began to melt soon after I began to pray, and the influence increased more and more during the whole sermon. The word seemed to pierce through and through, and carried such conviction with it that many, who before had industriously spoken evil of me, were ashamed of themselves. (Boston) Preached with great power, at Dr. Sewall's meeting-house, which was so exceedingly thronged, that I was obliged to get in at one of the windows.... I preached my farewell sermon to near twenty thousand people, . . . It being near dusk before I had done, the sight was more solemn. Numbers, great numbers, melted into tears when I talked of leaving them. I was very particular in my application, both to rulers, ministers, and people, and exhorted my hearers steadily to imitate the piety of their forefathers; so that I might hear, that with one heart and mind, they were striving together for the faith of the gospel. (Brookfield) Preached, with a little freedom at first, but, at the last, many were melted down. After dinner, was much enlarged and strengthened to wrestle strongly with God, for a revival of his work in these parts. (Suffield) ... preached at eleven o'clock to several thousands of people. I insisted much in my discourse upon the doctrine of the new birth, and also of the necessity of a minister being converted before he could preach Christ aright. The word came with great power, and a strong impression was made upon the people in all parts of the assembly. Many ministers were present. I did not spare them. (Northampton, at Jonathan Edward's Church) Preached this morning, and good Mr. Edwards wept during the whole time of exercise. The people were equally affected; and, in the afternoon, the power increased yet more. Our Lord seemed to keep the good wine till the last. I have not seen four such gracious meetings together since my arrival. Oh, that my soul may be refreshed with the joyful news, that Northampton people have recovered their first love; that the Lord has revived his work in their souls, and caused them to do their first works! (November, in New York) Preached in the morning with some freedom, but was dejected before the evening sermon, and when I came into the pulpit, I could have chosen to be silent rather than speak. After I had begun, however, the Spirit of the Lord gave me freedom, and at length came down like a mighty rushing wind, and carried all before it. Immediately, the whole congregation was alarmed. Crying, weeping, and wailing were to be heard in every corner; men's hearts failing them for fear, . . . My soul was carried out till I could scarce speak any more. (Baskinridge) . . . I had not discoursed long, when, and every part of the congregation, someone or another began to cry out, and almost all were melted into tears. A little boy, about eight years of age, wept as though his heart would break. . . . As I was going away, I asked the little boy what he cried for? He answered, his sins. I then asked what he wanted? He answered, Christ. (Philadelphia) It would be almost endless to recount all the particular instances of God's grace which I have seen this past week. Many who before were only convinced, now plainly prove that they were converted. My chief business now was to build up and to exhort them to continue in the grace of God. . . . Several Societies are now in the town, not only of men and women, but of little boys and little girls. (Maryland) Preached in the afternoon to about two thousand, and have not seen a more solid melting, I think, since my arrival. Some scoffers stood on the outside, but the Holy Spirit enabled me to lay the terrors of the Lord before them, and they grew more serious. (December, at Reed Island) This morning, the wind springing up fair, we set sail from Reed Island. But before I go on, stop, O my soul, and look back a little on the great things the Lord has done for thee during this excursion. I think it is now the seventy-fifth day since I arrived at Rhode Island. My body was then weak, but the Lord has much renewed its strength. I've been enabled to preach, I think, one hundred and seventy-five times in public, besides exhorting very frequently in private. I have traveled upwards of eight hundred miles and have gotten upwards of seven hundred pounds sterling in goods, provisions, and money for my orphans. Never did God vouchsafe me such great assistance. Never did I perform my journeys with so little fatigue, or see such a continuance of the Divine Presence in the congregations, to whom I have preached. All things concur to convince me that America is to be my chief scene for action. (Departed mid-January from Charleston, South Carolina, for England)[7]

---

7. Whitefield, *George Whitefield's Journals*, 343–505.

Historian Robert H. Lescenlius captured this season of divine favor noting that through the preaching of Whitefield, "the Spirit moved with conviction upon men. Without 'invitations,' personal workers, or decision cards, men were converted and leaped to make it known, or struggled under the power of conviction until they came to faith under the counsel of their pastors or on their own. He thundered against an unconverted ministry, and preachers were converted as well."[8] Like all seasons, the revival that began in Philadelphia in November of 1739 and subsequently spread like wildfire throughout the Middle Colonies, South, and again in New England, softened to a glow as Whitefield set sail to England in January of 1741. Although the next three decades would find Whitefield back in America an additional five times, most would agree that the later visits would not know the intensity that was reserved uniquely for the 1739 to1740 tour.

Throughout the intermittent years between missionary ventures to America, Whitefield was in Scotland fourteen times, with perhaps the best remembered trip being the historic revival at Cambuslang that commenced early in 1742. Additional journeys were made to Wales, where in 1741 he was wed to Elizabeth James. A fruit of their union was the birth of their only child, an infant son, who sadly died at the tender age of four months. England continued to experience grace as God opened doors for Whitefield to preach periodically among his native kinsmen. Later trips were made to Ireland, Portugal, Holland, and Bermuda. He was to complete his earthly pilgrimage at Newburyport, Massachusetts, on September 30, 1770. History records the late September evening concluded with a devotional meditation provided by Whitefield to a small gathering from the stairs of the parsonage where he was staying. This was to be his last formal message, for by seven the next morning he was absent from the body, but present with the Lord.

At this present juncture perhaps you may feel as though the Great Awakening had just lost its captain. For readers who share this sentiment, a necessary word must be said concerning the human tendency to place hope in a creature, rather than the Creator in whom we live, move, and have our being. Certainly, it is valiant men and women, such as George Whitefield, whom the Creator is often pleased to use to advance his kingdom; but all the bounty, all the mercy, all the conviction and vast heavenly power that accompanies these divine seasons of spiritual awakening are from God, and God alone! Servants will lose their human prowess, and eventually die;

---

8. Lescelius, "The Great Awakening" *Reformation and Revival Journal* 4, 3:32.

the eternal God of revival never tires or grows weary, and all he ordains to come to pass throughout each and every era of human history he will effortlessly achieve. When one Christian servant departs this earth or is called to a new field of service, our God most adequately raises up another, and then another, perhaps even you, to take their place and accomplish his purposes. A few additional stories to illustrate this great truth will conclude the present chapter. Read now of gospel servants, not the renowned but the ordinary, whom the extraordinary God was pleased to raise up for such a time as this, and renew your hope!

For the sake of space, the following narratives have been limited to Christian ministers who were serving in America around the time of Whitefield, but quite apart from his immediate influence. The discerning reader, however, will quickly notice that the God of Whitefield was likewise with them, and thus the fruit born through their service displays the same heavenly qualities. Undeniably, the Great Awakening was unfolding throughout this golden century on both sides of the Atlantic through the ministries of many who did not bear the name Whitefield or Wesley. In this regard we could accurately assume the gospel messengers represented next had counterparts too numerous to count not only in America, but also scattered throughout Europe and beyond. Consider, by means of illustration, the following narrative composed by Mr. Rowland, a Minister at Hopewell, who writes of an experience that occurred *prior* to Whitefield's arrival to New England in the Fall of 1739:

> [I]n Oct. sixth, 1739, there met about fifteen persons, eleven of whom were deeply convinced of their misery, and some of them cried out so very awfully, that I was constrained to conclude. After sermon I took an opportunity to enquire of those persons, what was the real cause of their crying out in such a manner? Some of whom answered me, "that they saw hell opening before them, and themselves ready to fall into it." Others answered me, "That they were struck with such a sense of their sinfulness, that they were afraid the Lord would never have mercy on them."[9]

The previous illustration represents a small gathering, compared to what was formerly reported of Whitefield's usual throng, yet who among us would not have savored such a moment as Rowland knew? And who among us, even with the best of our preparation, is humanly capable of creating a climate where conviction flows so freely? Only God! Read

9. Gillies, *Historical Collections of Accounts of Revival*, 338.

again of God's work *following* a seemingly ineffective message preached at an Elizabethtown parish by George Whitefield, so that the joy of revival might be reserved for the faithful Mr. Dickinson who served as the parish rector. His story follows:

> The Rev. Mr. Whitefield preached a sermon here in the fall of the year 1739, to a numerous and attentive auditory; but I could observe no further influence upon our people by that address, than a general thoughtfulness about religion; . . . To that end, there were frequent lectures appointed to the young people in particular; but without any visible success, until sometime in June 1740, when we had a remarkable manifestation of the divine presence among us. Having at that time invited the young people to hear a sermon, there was a numerous congregation convened, which consisted chiefly of our youth, though there were many others with them. I preached them a plain, practical sermon; without any special liveliness or vigor; for I was then in a remarkably dead and dull frame, till enlivened by a sudden and deep impression which visibly appeared upon the congregation in general. . . . the inward distress and concern of the audience discovered itself by their tears, and by an audible sobbing and sighing in almost all parts of the assembly. There appeared such tokens of a solemn and deep concern, as I never before saw in any congregation whatsoever. From this time, we heard no more of our young people's meeting together for frolics and extravagant diversions, as had been usual among them; but instead thereof, private meetings for religious exercises were by them set up in several parts of the town.[10]

A few more accounts will be shared lest they are forgotten in the pages of history and the joy they impart lost from our hearts. Walk with me, one final time, though the soft hills of New England as the Spirit of God, in one soul and then yet another, rescues the dying lives of those who in earlier years inhabited this budding nation.

> (Mr. Seccomb, Minister at Harvard) The work of conviction and conversion was begun and carried on in a gradual manner, principally, by the preaching of the word. The preached word became more quick and powerful than usual; like as a fire, and like a hammer that breaketh the rock in pieces. (Mr. Samuel Blair, Minister at New Londonderry[11]) The number of the awakened increased very fast; frequently under sermons there were some newly convicted,

---

10. Gillies, *Historical Collections of Accounts of Revival*, 340.
11. As was previously cited, a sermon by Samuel Blair is furnished in appendix two.

and brought into deep distress of soul about their perishing estate. Our Sabbath assemblies soon became vastly large. (Mr. Prince from Boston reporting on his experience as well as those of his colleagues) The Rev. Mr. Cooper was wont to say, that more came to him in one week in deep concern about their souls than in the whole twenty-four years of his preceding ministry. I can also say the same as to the numbers who repaired to me. By Mr. Cooper's letter to his friend in Scotland, it appears, as he has had about six hundred different persons in three months' time, and Mr. Webb informs me, he has had in the same space above a thousand. (Mr. Crocker, Minister at Taunton) I think I never saw such an assembly before; such awful reverence, such serious concern of mind, under the word. (Mr. Parsons, Minister of the West Parish of Lyme) . . . I do not remember that I preached a sermon through the month, without some manifest tokens of the presence of God in our assemblies. . . . People flocked to my study daily, and in great numbers, deeply wounded, . . . Sometimes I had thirty in a day; and sometimes many more, all upon the grand affairs of their souls. (Mr. Thatcher, Minister in Middleborough) From this time there was an uncommon teachableness among my people, scarce one word of counsel seemed lost, or a sermon in vain.[12]

We will now depart from the shores of America and return to the familiar soil of England, where another renowned gospel minister, John Wesley, was being summoned by our sovereign God to serve as a principal messenger through whom much of England would be set ablaze with the fire of revival. It is not to his later years that we will initially turn, but to his earliest. In this way, as with Whitefield, we can delight in observing the divine calling unfold in the life of one whose name is also readily identified with the event known as the First Great Awakening. Turn the page and join me in England during the summer of 1703 where a young son named John had just been born to Samuel and Susanna Wesley.

---

12. Gillies, *Historical Collections of Accounts of Revival*, 341–420.

5

England Ablaze!

MORE THAN A DECADE before the birth of George Whitefield, the God of history had planted another seed of blessing in the parched European soil. This seed was John Wesley. To those who surrounded the Wesley home on June 28, 1703, the birth of young John may have also appeared as merely a family blessing. God had different plans, however, for in a few brief decades the name and work of this child of noble promise would be known throughout England and beyond. Differing from the inn where Whitefield was born, Wesley's birth occurred in a rectory at Epworth where his father served as the vicar. The following prayer, recorded by his mother, readily displays the piety evident within the Wesley home, "I do intend to be more particularly careful of the soul of this child that Thou hast so mercifully provided for, than ever I have been; that I may endeavor to instill into his mind Thy principles of true religion and virtue."[1]

Despite the spiritual training in his early years, young Wesley embraced a misguided belief that one achieved justification before God based upon personal virtue and outward expressions of religious devotion, rather than by faith in the substitutionary atoning sacrifice of Jesus Christ. In this regard, he records the following thoughts written during his teenage years, "And what I now hoped to be saved by, was, (1) not being as bad as other people, (2) having still a kindness for religion, and (3) reading the Bible, going to church and saying my prayers."[2] The fruit of his inward devotion, although earnest in intention, produced a conflicted soul that remained "almost continually guilty of outward sins, which I knew to be such, though they were not scandalous in the eyes of the world."[3]

---

1. Wood, *The Burning Heart*, 31.
2. Wesley, *The Journal of John Wesley*, 1:465
3. Wesley, *The Journal of John Wesley*, 1:465–466.

A week after his seventeenth birthday, John entered Oxford University and over the course of the next eight years was ordained a deacon, and then a priest, in the Church of England. On March 17, 1726, he was elected a Fellow of Lincoln College where he maintained a "continued endeavored to keep the whole law, inward and outward . . . including visiting the prisons, assisting the poor and sick in town, and doing what other good I could."[4] When reflecting on these years of exhausting self-denial and dutiful service Wesley writes, "I could not find that all this gave me any comfort or assurance of acceptance with God."[5] Like Whitefield before him, he had yet to know "a union of the soul with God."[6]

To satisfy his longing to discover acceptance from God, John pursued a missionary endeavor among the American Indians in 1735 that proved to be, according to his *Journal*, a distressing failure. On his return passage to England, however, Wesley was divinely introduced to a group of Moravian missionaries who were fellow travelers on the same ship. He was particularly impressed by their genuine faith and calmness of spirit during a perilous time on the voyage. The initial encounter on board the ship led to a dialogue with Moravian leader, August Gottlieb Spangenberg, who, along with the other brethren in his fellowship, had an abiding assurance of salvation the Oxford scholar painfully lacked. Upon his return to England additional meetings were secured with various other Moravians where Wesley urgently sought to understand how he might discover the inward peace they so obviously knew.

The spiritual breakthrough finally came on May 24, 1738, at a small religious society that met on Aldersgate Street. This society, though sponsored by the Anglicans, displayed the marks of Moravian influence. It was in this setting that he heard a reading from Martin Luther's preface to Romans, where the great theological doctrine of justification by faith alone was clearly articulated. Through the enablement of the Holy Spirit, this truth produced a converting influence in the soul of John Wesley. He describes the moment of his awakening in the following words:

> In the evening I went unwillingly to a society in Aldersgate Street, where one was reading Luther's preface to the Epistle to the Romans. About a quarter before nine, while he was describing the change which God works in the heart through faith in Christ, I felt

---

4. Wesley, *The Journal of John Wesley*, 1:467.
5. Wesley, *The Journal of John Wesley*, 1:468.
6. Wesley, *The Journal of John Wesley*, 1:469.

my heart strangely warmed. I felt I did trust in Christ, Christ alone, for salvation and assurance was given me that he had taken away my sins, even mine, and saved me from the law of sin and death.[7]

With overflowing joy, Wesley also now knew "a union of the soul with God" that three years earlier had transformed the life of George Whitefield. Again, like Whitefield before him, the preaching of Wesley was now often graced by the anointing of the Spirit.[8] The following testimony from Wesley will illustrate this claim:

> From 1738 to this time (1746)—speaking continually of Jesus Christ, laying Him only for the foundation of the whole building, making Him all in all, the first and the last, preaching only on this plan, "the kingdom of God is at hand, repent ye and believe in the gospel," the word of God ran as fire among the stubble, it was glorified more and more; multitudes crying out, "What must we do to be saved?" and, afterwards witnessed, "by grace we are saved through faith."[9]

In April of 1739, the same God of history who had tenderly guarded John Wesley's life throughout the deep inner trials of his early years was ready to present him with a new and formidable challenge. The challenge was prompted through George Whitefield, who was found on the hillsides surrounding the city of Bristol tirelessly proclaiming the gospel. The reader may recall that at this point in history the Great Awakening was gaining momentum on both sides of the Atlantic, with Whitefield serving as its primary evangelist. The reader may likewise remember that during this general era Whitefield had moved his pulpit from the familiar, but now forbidden, conventional English sanctuary to the open fields situated beneath the sanctuary of God's spacious heaven. Wesley records in his *Journal*, early in the spring of 1739, his initial impression of Whitefield's choice spot of exposition:

> In the evening I reached Bristol and met Mr. Whitefield there. I could scarce reconcile myself at first to this strange way of preaching in the fields, of which he set me an example on Sunday; having been all my life (until very lately) so tenacious of every point

---

7. Wesley, *The Journal of John Wesley*, 1:475–476.

8. A sermon by John Wesley titled *The Way to the Kingdom* is furnished in appendix one.

9. Wesley, *The Letters of the Rev. John Wesley*, 2:264.

relating to decency and order, that I should have thought the saving of souls almost a sin if it had not been done in a church.[10]

One could hardly overlook the sovereign blessing God bestowed on the preaching of Whitefield as literally thousands gathered in the open countryside to hear the saving message of the gospel of Christ. This initial impression prompted Wesley to step up to the hillside pulpit the following afternoon, a practice he was often to repeat from this day forward, where a vast number of spiritually thirsty souls welcomed his presence. He describes the moment in his *Journal:*

> At four in the afternoon I submitted to be more vile and proclaimed in the highways the glad tidings of salvation, speaking from a little eminence in a ground adjoining to the city, to about three thousand people. The Scripture on which I spoke was this, (is it possible any one should be ignorant that it is fulfilled in every true minister of Christ?), "The Spirit of the Lord is upon me, because he hath anointed me to preach the gospel to the poor. He hath sent me to heal the broken-hearted; to preach deliverance to the captives, and recovery of sight to the blind; to set at liberty them that are bruised, to proclaim the acceptable year of the Lord."[11]

Although the previous year had provided Wesley with numerous opportunities to preach, church doors were also increasingly closed to him, which solidified his adoption of Whitefield's chosen style of proclamation throughout 1739 and beyond. Indeed, the fact that this meticulous and orthodox clergyman did venture "into the highways and by-ways and face the great unwashed was nothing short of a miracle."[12] When writing a letter to Samuel Walker, who served as the curate at St. Mary, Truro, John Wesley suggested his reluctant decision to adopt field preaching was based primarily upon irreconcilable doctrinal differences with the established church. To this end he writes:

> [T]he reproach (from the Church) . . . was abundantly increased when we began to preach repentance and remission of sins and insist that we are justified by faith. For this cause were we excluded from preaching in the churches (I say, for *this*, as yet there was

---

10. Wesley, *The Journal of John Wesley*, 2:167.
11. Wesley, *The Journal of John Wesley*, 2:172–173.
12. Wood, *The Burning Heart*, 94.

no field-preaching). And this exclusion occasioned our preaching elsewhere, with the other irregularities that followed.[13]

The historical accounts following Wesley's break from traditional church methodology demonstrate that the Son, whose merciful light was now spreading throughout Europe in brilliant glory, continued to bestow his sovereign blessing on both the message and method of his servant. Similar to Whitefield's great missionary tours in America, the ministry of Wesley throughout the remainder of this precious year was likewise graced with the unction and power of the Spirit. By means of illustration, read the following accounts from the *Journal* of John Wesley, and observe with reverential joy the footprints of God walking again among the nations, setting portions of England and Wales ablaze with spiritual fire.

> (April, 1739) At seven in the morning I preached to about a thousand persons at Bristol, and afterwards to about fifteen hundred on the top of Hanham Mount in Kingswood. . . . About five thousand were in the afternoon at Rose Garden. . . . I was desired to go to Bath, where I offered to about a thousand souls the free grace of God to "heal their backsliding"; and in the morning to (I believe) more than two thousand. . . . I preached at the Poorhouse; three or four hundred were within, and more than twice that number without. . . . On Easter day, it being a thorough rain, I could only preach at Newgate at eight in the morning and two in the afternoon, in a house near Hanham Mount at eleven, and in one near Rose Garden at five. At the society in the evening many were cut to the heart, and many comforted. . . . While I was preaching at Newgate . . . immediately one, and another, and another sunk to the earth; they dropped on every side as thunderstruck. . . . One was so wounded by the sword of the Spirit that you could have imagined she could not live a moment. (May) As I was expounding in the Black Lane on the righteousness of the Scribes and Pharisees . . . two, who seem to be more deeply convinced than the rest, did not long sorrow as men without hope, but found in that hour that they had "an advocate with the Father, Jesus Christ the righteous"; as did three others in Gloucester Lane the evening before, and three at Baldwin Street this evening. . . . At Weavers Hall a woman first, and then a boy about fourteen years of age, were overwhelmed with sin, and sorrow, and fear. But we cried to God, and their souls were delivered. . . . Today . . . our Lord answered for himself. For while I was enforcing these words, "Be still, and know that I am

---

13. Wesley, *The Letters of the Rev. John Wesley*, 3:225.

God," he began to make bare his arm, not in a close room, neither in private, but in the open air, and before more than two thousand witnesses. One, and another, and another was struck to the earth, exceedingly trembling at the presence of his power. Others cried with a loud and bitter cry, "what must we do to be saved?" . . . I preached, at the Rose Green . . . to the largest congregation I ever had there; I believe upwards of ten thousand souls . . . (June) Many came to me and earnestly advised me not to preach abroad in the afternoon, because there was a combination of several persons who threatened terrible things. This report being spread abroad brought many thither of the better sort of people (so called), and added, I believe, more than a thousand to the ordinary congregation. . . . The power of God came with his word, so that none scoffed, or interrupted, or opened his mouth. . . . I preached at Priestdown . . . In the midst of the prayer after sermon, two men (hired, as we afterwards understood, for that purpose) began singing a ballad. After a few mild words . . . used without effect, we all began singing a psalm which put them entirely to silence. We then poured out our souls in prayer for them, and they appeared altogether confounded. . . . I went with Mr. Whitfield to Blackheath where were, I believe, twelve to fourteen thousand people. He a little surprised me by desiring me to preach in his stead, which I did (though nature recoiled), on my favorite subject, "Jesus Christ, who of God is made unto us wisdom, righteousness, sanctification, and redemption." . . . Three persons terribly felt the wrath of God abiding on them at the society this evening; but, upon prayer made in their behalf, he was pleased soon to lift up the light of his countenance upon them. (July) I went to a gentleman who was much troubled with what they call lowness of spirits. Many such have I been with before, but in several of them it was no bodily distemper. They wanted something, they knew not what, and were therefore heavy, uneasy, and dissatisfied with everything. The plain truth is that they wanted God, they wanted Christ, they wanted faith, and God convince them of their want in a way that their physicians no more understood than themselves. Accordingly, nothing availed until the Great Physician came. For, in spite of all natural means, he who made them for himself could not suffer them to rest until they rested in him. . . . We had an attentive congregation at Gloucester in the evening. In the morning . . . I preached to about five thousand . . . It rained violently at five in the evening; notwithstanding which, two or three thousand people stayed. (August) I preached . . . to about two thousand persons. . . Some of them mocked at first, whom I reproved before all, and those of them who stayed were more serious. Several spoke to me after who were, for the present, much affected. . . . I had the satisfaction of conversing with a Quaker, and afterwards with an Anabaptist, who, I trust, have had a large measure of the love of God shed abroad in their hearts. Oh may those, in every persuasion, who are of this spirit increase a thousandfold, how many soever they be! . . . My mouth was opened and my heart enlarged strongly to declare to above two thousand people at Bradford that "the kingdom of God" within us "is not meat and drink, but righteousness, and peace, and joy in the Holy Ghost." (September) I talked largely with my mother who told me that till a short time since, she had scarce heard such a thing mentioned as the having forgiveness of sins now, or God's spirit bearing witness with our spirit; much less did she imagine that this was the common privilege of all true believers. "Therefore," she said, "I never did ask for it myself. But two or three weeks ago, while my son Hall was pronouncing these words in delivering the cup to me, 'the blood of our Lord Jesus Christ, which was given for thee,' the words struck through my heart, and I knew God for Christ's sake had forgiven *me* all *my* sins." . . . I declared to about ten thousand, in Moorfields, what they must do to be saved. My mother went with us, about five, to Kennington, where were supposed to be twenty thousand people. . . . From Kennington I went to a society at Lambeth. The house being filled, the rest stood in the garden. The deep attention they showed me gave a good hope that they will not all be forgetful hearers. . . . I went in the afternoon to a society at Deptford, and then at six came to Turner's hall, which holds (by computation) two thousand persons. The press both within and without was very great. . . . (October) . . . At five in the evening I explained to about a thousand people the nature, the cause, and the condition or instrument of justification, . . . Between five and six I called on all who were present (about three thousand) at Stanley, on the green near the town, to accept Christ as their only "wisdom, righteousness, sanctification, and redemption." . . . About eight I reached Hampton Common . . . There were, it was computed, five or six thousand persons. . . . On Wednesday the spirit of many revived; on Thursday evening many more found him in whom they had believed to be "a present help in time of trouble." And never do I remember the power of God to have been more eminently present than this morning, . . . (October in Wales) About a thousand people stood patiently (though the frost was sharp, it being after sunset) while, from Acts 28:22, I simply described the plain old religion of the Church of England, which is now almost everywhere spoken against, under the new name of Methodism. . . . When I came to Pontypool in the afternoon, being unable to procure any more convenient place, I stood in the street, and cried aloud to five or six hundred attentive hearers . . . Many were melted to tears. . . . At four I preached at the Shire Hall of Cardiff . . . At six almost the whole town (I was informed) came together, to whom I explained the six last Beatitudes; but my heart was so enlarged I knew not how to give it over, so that we continued three hours. Oh, may the seed they have received have its fruit under holiness, and in the end everlasting life! [14]

In his critique of this extraordinary year, historian Luke Tyerman writes:

With the exception of a brief visit to London in June, September, and November, and of a short tour into Wales and another to Exeter, Wesley spent the whole of his time, from April to the end of 1739, in Bristol and its immediate neighborhood; but, at different times, he rendered important service in other places . . . it is not too much to say that he delivered at least five hundred discourses and expositions in the nine months of which we speak; and it is a noticeable fact that only eight of those were delivered in the churches.[15]

Throughout 1739 and beyond, Wesley also developed the formal structure of the well-known Great Awakening *societies*, adding a different small group model in 1742 identified as *classes*. Due to their prominent place in the Awakening, and particularly throughout England, I have provided a detailed synopsis of each of these two group structures in the next chapter. It is my opinion that the spiritual fruit of the Great Awakening, while primarily initiated and sustained by the sovereign and omnipotent Spirit of God, was significantly nourished through the spiritual disciplines fostered in these groups. In fact, when Wesley departed this earth in 1791 there were no less than 72,000 members registered in the Great Britain societies alone, not counting those in America![16]

As the calendar of history turns to 1740, Wesley finds himself increasingly at odds with numerous clergy, some members of his immediate family, and sadly with his comrade in ministry, George Whitefield.[17] Elder

14. Wesley, *The Journal of John Wesley*, 2:175–296.

15. Tyerman, *The Life of The Reverend John Wesley*, combination of related quotations on 1:234 and 1:282.

16. Wood, *The Burning Heart*, 114.

17. An accounting of the schism and eventual healing that ensued between John

brother Samuel Wesley, for example, was strongly opposed to the work of both Charles and John throughout his entire life. In a letter to his mother concerning the ministry of his siblings Samuel emphatically declared, "it was with exceeding concern and grief, I heard you had countenanced a spreading delusion . . . Is it not enough that I am bereft of both my brothers, but must my mother follow too?"[18] The Vicar of Christ Church in London, Joseph Trapp, expressed a similar disdain for both the men and their doctrines through a lengthy pamphlet where he exhorted all of England to "go not after these impostors and seducers; but shun them as you would the plague."[19] History reveals that the opinions of Trapp were also embraced by an ever widening circle of clergy.

Moving beyond the difficult year of 1740, we enter a more favorable season where the revival Spirit was again advancing with power, converting souls by the score. As part of God's sovereign plan, a new host of volunteers were being assembled to assist in cultivating the growing spiritual harvest. The volunteers to whom I refer were the controversial non-ordained *lay preachers* who came alongside the ordained clergy to serve as evangelists, teachers, and spiritual leaders within the growing Methodist movement. The reader may recall from the previous chapter titled *First Lights,* there were lay preachers busy in the Lord's fields well before the actual genesis of the Awakening, such as Howell Harris of Wales. John Wesley added other eminent personalities to their ranks, including John Cennick and Thomas Maxfield, offering the following justification for his decision, "I know no Scripture which forbids making use of such help, in a case of such necessity. And I praise God who has given even this help to those poor sheep, when 'their own shepherds pitied them not.'"[20] Had the ordained clergy been more attentive to the masses, chides Wesley, perhaps this great influx of laity in various fields of Christian service would not have been quite as necessary. In fact, the thousands of societies and classes that were developed throughout this common era were primarily facilitated through the efforts of devoted laity.

As volunteer ministry was expanding throughout 1741, the omnipotent Lord was likewise rejuvenating the Awakening through the persistent ministry of Wesley and his disciples. From June to December of that year,

---

Wesley and George Whitefield can be found in the prefatory notes of appendix one.

18. Tyerman, *The Life of The Reverend John Wesley,* 1:286.
19. Tyerman, *The Life of The Reverend John Wesley,* 1:242.
20. Tyerman, *The Life of The Reverend John Wesley,* 1:371.

the following entries in the *Journal* of Wesley attest to the rekindled Holy Spirit fire, again setting portions of England and Wales ablaze through the sovereign decree of God.

> (June) I exhorted a crowded congregation not to "receive the grace of God in vain." The same exhortation I enforced on the society (about nine hundred persons); and by their fruits it doth appear that they begin to love one another, "not in word" only, "but in deed and in truth." . . . I preached in the morning on the inward kingdom of God. And many, I trust, found they were heathens in heart, and Christians in name only. . . . Thence I went to Hemington, where also, the house not being large enough to contain the people, they stood about the door and at both the windows, while I showed "what" we "must do to be saved." . . . I rode to Nottingham again, and at eight preached at the market-place . . . to an immense multitude of people . . . I saw only one or two who behaved lightly, whom I immediately spoke to, and they stood reproved. . . . (July) The school at Kingswood was thoroughly filled between eight and nine in the evening. I showed them from the example of the Corinthians what need we have to bear one with another . . . We then poured out our souls in prayer and praise, and our Lord did not hide his face from us. . . . It being my turn (which comes about once in three years), I preached at St. Mary's before the University. The harvest truly is plenteous. So numerous a congregation (from whatever motives they came) I have seldom seen at Oxford. (August) The body of our sister Muncy being brought to Short's Gardens . . . where I performed the last office in the presence of such an innumerable multitude of people as I never saw gathered together before. (September) I met about two hundred persons, with whom severally I had talked the week before, at the French chapel in Hermitage Street. . . . I preached in Charles Square, Hoxton . . . I trust God blessed his word. The scoffers stood abashed, and opened not their mouth. . . . In the evening we went to Kingswood. The House was filled from end to end. And we continued in ministering the word of God, in prayer and praise, till the morning. (October, ministering in Wales jointly with Howell Harris and Daniel Rowlands) At three we went to church. There was a vast congregation, though at only a few hours' warning. . . . I road to Wenvoe. The church was thoroughly filled with attentive hearers. . . . At eleven I preached at the prison . . . In the afternoon I was desired to meet one of the honorable women, whom I found a mere sinner, groaning under the mighty hand of God. . . . (October in England) I got to Kingswood by two. The words God enabled me to speak there, and afterwards at Bristol . . . were as a hammer and a flame;

and the same blessing we found at the meeting of the society, but more abundantly at the lovefeast which followed. I remember nothing like it for many months. A cry was heard from one end of the congregation to the other; not of grief, but of overflowing joy and love. (November–December, with much of November and some of December spent recovering from ailments) . . . I walked over to Bath, and had a conversation of several hours with one who had lived above seventy, and studied divinity above thirty years, yet remission of sins was quite a new doctrine to him. But I trust God will write it on his heart. . . . The morning congregation was increased to above thrice the usual number, . . . At Long Lane likewise, in the evening, I had a crowded audience. . .[21]

A continued examination of the *Journal* through 1742 and beyond will provide the reader with added joy as they peruse the gracious stories describing the hand of God, in both powerful and quiet seasons, working through the lives of his chosen instruments to reclaim the soul of this once decedent nation. I believe historian A. Skevington Wood was correct when he stated that John Wesley "was destined to be an evangelist. Along with George Whitefield and his own brother, Charles, he was called of God to lead the mission to Britain. Within twenty years, however, Charles was to retire almost completely from active campaigning. Whitefield died in 1770, worn out by his herculean labors. But John battled on for over fifty years, and lived to see the tide turned and a nation awakened."[22]

As the narratives of the remaining decades that John Wesley and his colleagues labored are studied, it is evident that throughout both Europe and America the tide of moral debauchery did in fact turn, and both nations were divinely awakened by the omnipotent sovereign hand of God. Yet while the human messengers who heralded the gospel throughout the Awakening were numerous, the task of organizing and refining various group structures to disciple the souls whom the Lord Christ had purchased was assigned primarily to John Wesley. Under his principal supervision three distinct styles of groups, the society, class, and band, were organized and implemented to promote the disciplines of evangelism, biblical study, faith-based living, accountable discipleship, and social service. Two of these groups, the society and class, contain many transferable principles contemporary Christian workers will likely find to be of value. The basic organizational structure of each is provided in the subsequent chapter.

21. Wesley, *The Journal of John Wesley*, 2:465–518.
22. Wood, *The Burning Heart*, 83.

6

Cultivating the Harvest

THROUGHOUT THE PREVIOUS CHAPTERS, the reader was introduced to accounts of genuine spiritual awakening that likely caused all pious hearts to yearn for a similar outpouring of divine favor in our present day. Unique to this season of historic revival, however, were the widespread groups developed or refined principally by Wesley to ensure the vast harvest of new converts were spiritually grounded in biblical truth. Generally speaking, there were two primary groups utilized to promote spiritual growth within the newly revived community of faith. The initial group was a larger gathering known as *societies*, with the second a smaller group identified as *classes*.

A close examination of the structure of these groups is of far more importance than mere historical interest, for even the most casual observer of contemporary Christianity would likely agree the average church would be notably strengthened if a majority of its members were routinely "seeking the power of godliness, united in order to pray together, to receive the word of exhortation, and to watch over one another in love, that they may help each other to work out their salvation."[1] These were the basic goals of the *United Societies*! Now suppose a majority of Christian believers *also* met weekly in a small group, under the leadership of a godly mentor, where the membership "now happily experienced that Christian fellowship of which they had not so much as an idea before. They began to 'bear one another's burdens,' and naturally to 'care for one another.' As they had daily a more intimate acquaintance with, so they had a more endeared affection for, each other. And 'speaking the truth in love,' they grew up into him in all things, who is the head, even Christ."[2] These were the experiences

---

1. Wesley, *The Works of John Wesley*, 8:269.
2. Wesley, *The Works of John Wesley*, 8:254.

commonly enjoyed by eighteenth-century Christians who gathered in the small groups known as *classes*!

Groups such as the *society* and *class*, however, were not just flourishing throughout the First Great Awakening, similar models were also were evident within the life of the early church. After the great revival best known as Pentecost, for example, many who experienced the converting power of the Spirit:

> ... devoted themselves to the apostles' teaching and the fellowship, to the breaking of bread and the prayers.... And all who believed were together and had all things in common. And they were selling their possessions and belongings and distributing the proceeds to all, as any had need. And day by day, attending the temple together and breaking bread in their homes, they received their food with glad and generous hearts, praising God and having favor with all the people. And the Lord added to their number day by day those who were being saved.[3]

The New Testament likewise registers small group meetings in the house of Mary (Acts 12:12), the jailer (Acts 16:32–34), Priscilla and Aquila (Rom 16:5), Nympha (Col 4:15), and Philemon (Phlm 2). In fact, according to historian Wayne A. Meeks, "the meeting places of the Pauline groups, and probably most other early Christian groups, were private homes."[4] It is my personal conviction that much of the *radical Christianity* apparent in the early church and throughout the First Great Awakening was cultivated in groups where the Scriptures were not only taught, but practiced; and would not such *radical Christianity* be pleasing to our God in this present hour? It is my hope that the reader would be inspired to not only study the two Great Awakening group models outlined in this chapter, but also appropriately adapt these models to their particular field of service so that the work of Christ might be similarly magnified and advanced.

The Society

The initial societies associated with the First Great Awakening were not introduced by Wesley, as some may assume, but by his colleague George Whitefield. In the early months of 1737, Whitefield records the following entry in his *Journal*, "I preached, as usual, about five times a week; but the

---

3. Acts 2:42–47, (ESV).
4. Meeks, *The First Urban Christians*, 75.

congregation grew, if possible, larger and larger. . . . Persons of all denominations flocked to hear. Persons of all ranks, not only publicly attended my ministry, but gave me private invitations to their houses. A private society or two were erected."[5]

The forming influences of the Great Awakening religious societies, however, predate both Whitefield and Wesley, and can be traced to various individuals including a seventeenth-century Anglican cleric by the name of Anthony Horneck.[6] Horneck's burden to improve the lax spiritual state of the church prompted him to encourage believers to meet regularly in small societies for the purpose of study, prayer, and mutual accountability. A copy of the *Orders* of one such society, which supply the reader with an insightful overview of the conduct required of group members, is furnished in appendix three. These early societies also cared for to the needy in their communities and were often involved in social service.[7]

The reader may recall from the chapter titled *First Lights* that Philip Jacob Spener was establishing Pietistic devotional groups in Germany during this same general era. Many of these European groups united to form consolidated associations, which included the *Society for Promoting Christian Knowledge*, also known as *SPCK*. The basic format of *SPCK* soon became a model for many of the local societies within Europe, including the society that gathered in the Epworth parish under the direction of John Wesley's father, Samuel Wesley.[8] Through a mixture of formal and informal exposure to such groups, John Wesley developed his own religious society design that became the standard model throughout the Awakening. An examination of this model will be surveyed next.

Beginnings

Chapter four detailed the account of Wesley's conversion and subsequent call to serve in Bristol alongside the maverick field preacher, George Whitefield. In response to God's omnipotent blessing, scores of converts were brought into the fold through the converting influence of the Holy Spirit and the faithful preaching of both men. When Whitefield returned to America in 1739, Wesley was placed in charge of the growing work in Bristol while

---

5. Whitefield, *George Whitefield's Journals*, 84.
6. Stoeffler, *Continental Pietism and Early American Christianity*, 185.
7. Heitzenrater, *Mirror and Memory*, 36–40.
8. Heitzenrater, *Wesley and the People Called Methodists*, 27–28.

still attending to the needs of his congregation in London. The rapid growth of the revival movement, combined with his divided ministerial duties, inspired Wesley to further develop, implement, and refine the society structure. As the societies under this administration grew in number, Wesley joined them under the title *United Societies*. In 1743 John and his brother Charles developed a set of written guidelines to govern the societies. These guidelines, titled *The Nature, Design, and General Rules of The United Societies*, are available in appendix three. The following is a review of various primary elements found within the United Society guidelines.

Size and Membership

Societies varied in size from just a few members to several hundred participants, with admission open to all who shared a desire "to flee from the wrath to come, to be saved from their sins."[9] The organizational format of the society provided a rich atmosphere for new and seasoned Christians alike to receive biblical teaching, vigorous challenge, and practical advice to aid their spiritual journey. Unbelievers who expressed an earnest yearning to "flee from the wrath to come" were also understood to have been welcomed at society gatherings. Society *membership*, however, was offered only to genuine Christians who wholeheartedly affirmed the *General Rules* of the United Societies and successfully completed a two-month trial observation under the oversight of an appointed leader.[10]

Organizational Structure

The *General Rules*, particularly sections four through six, illustrate many of the biblical principles that shaped the organizational structure of the society. By means of illustration, in the *Rules* Wesley instructs faithful society members to care for "all men" and to serve both the Christian and non-Christian communities "by giving food to the hungry, by clothing the naked, by visiting or helping them that are sick, or in prison—to their souls, by instructing, reproving, or exhorting."[11] The priority of mutual accountability expected from society members is also evident. In the eyes of Wesley

---

9. Wesley, *The Works of John Wesley*, 8:270.
10. Wesley, *The Works of John Wesley*, 8:307.
11. Wesley, *The Works of John Wesley*, 8:271.

and the New Testament writers alike, religion was not exclusively a private concern. From its beginning, the society was to be "a company of men" who intend "to watch over one another in love, that they may help each other work out their salvation."[12]

A vigilant study of the Bible, among other disciplines, was likewise an expectation for both the members and their leaders. To this end, the *General Rules* mandate all society members "should continue to evidence their desire of salvation . . . by attending upon all the ordinances of God. Such are, the public worship of God, the ministry of the word, either read or expounded, the Supper of the Lord, family and private prayer, searching the Scriptures, and fasting, or abstinence."[13] It was the leaders, however, who were expected to be "a master of theology, well acquainted with the sacred Scriptures, having lucid views of doctrinal truth, of Christian experience, and of moral and religious duties. In order to teach, he must learn; to attain this, he should study well."[14]

To enforce these various disciplines, the general membership was examined weekly by their class leader, and quarterly by the preacher or assistant assigned to their district.[15] Undoubtedly these routine evaluations provided a context where biblical truths were presented, questions were answered, insights received, reproof shared, encouragement experienced, and the bread of fellowship enjoyed. The routine evaluation of society members was so significant to the Wesley brothers that they assumed ultimate responsibility to ensure its fulfillment. To this end they write:

> If there be any among us who observe them [the *General Rules*] not, who habitually break any of them, let it be made known unto him who watches over their soul as they that must give an account. We will admonish him of the error of his ways, we will bear with him for a season; But then if he repent not, he hath no more place among us. We have delivered our own souls.[16]

The evangelism, social service, mutual accountability, scriptural study, and faith-based living practiced by many faithful society members no doubt furnished a stark contrast to the idle religion that existed among a majority of the European populace. Christians were once again, as in

---

12. Wesley, *The Works of John Wesley*, 8:269.
13. Wesley, *The Works of John Wesley*, 8:271.
14. Watson, *The Early Methodists Class Meeting*, 102–103.
15. Wesley, *The Works of John Wesley*, 8:270, 8:305-307, 8:319–320.
16. Wesley, *The Works of John Wesley*, 8:271.

the days following Pentecost, identified by their biblical lifestyle and orthodox profession of faith!

The Class

To further assist with the spiritual oversight of every society member, small groups were soon formed *within* the larger societies. These small groups, identified as *classes*, were introduced in the early part of 1742. Wesley describes the genesis of the idea in a portion of the following letter to his intimate friend, Vincent Perronet:

> I was talking with several of the Society in Bristol concerning the means of paying the debts here, when one stood up and said, "let every member of the Society give a penny a week till all are paid." Another answered, "But many of them are poor, and cannot afford it . . . "Then," said he, "put eleven of the poorest with me; and if they can give anything, well, I will call on them weekly; and if they can give nothing, I will give for them as well as for myself. And each of you call on eleven of your neighbors weekly; receive what they give, and make up what is wanting." It was done. In a while, some of these informed me, they found such and such a one did not live as he ought. It struck me immediately. "This is the thing, the very thing we have wanted so long." I called together all the leaders of the classes (so we used to term them and their companies), and desired that each would make a particular inquiry into the behavior of those whom he saw weekly. They did so. Many disorderly walkers were detected. Some turned from the evil of their ways. Some were put away from us. Many saw it with fear and rejoiced unto God with reverence.[17]

Although the class leaders initially fulfilled their pastoral oversight through weekly house-to-house visitation, it soon became evident that individual home visitation was not always possible, and at times inconvenient. In place of home visitation, the leader requested their members meet together weekly in the context of a small group, and thus the classes were born! It was in the context of these gatherings that "advice or reproof was given as need required, quarrels made up, misunderstandings removed; and after an hour or two spent in this labour of love, they concluded with prayer and thanksgiving."[18] The classes, along with the so-

---

17. Wesley, *The Letters of the Rev. John Wesley*, 2:296.
18. Wesley, *The Letters of the Rev. John Wesley*, 2:297.

cieties, likely served as the primary framework through which the Holy Spirit developed and maintained many of the biblical principles of renewal throughout the Awakening.

Size and Membership

Classes averaged around a dozen members and commonly met weekly in the homes of fellow society attenders who lived within a shared topographical region. The composition of classes varied; some were sorted by age, some by marital status, while others were divided strictly by gender.[19] Every person who belonged to a society was also expected to be an active member of a class, and each class member was expected to faithfully adhere to the disciplines of their group. Such disciplines included regular attendance, accountability for personal and spiritual growth as outlined in the *Rules of the United Societies*, along with weekly contributions given according to their means. The group and individual disciplines were, as was noted previously, strictly enforced through both weekly and quarterly examinations. The class members who were found to be spiritually faithful in both word and deed were issued a quarterly ticket. This ticket renewed their group membership and granted admittance to the love feast [communion service] and society meetings.[20] Those who were found to be "disorderly members" were removed in a "quiet and inoffensive" manner from class membership.[21]

Organizational Structure

As historical descriptions of typical class meetings are studied, they readily reveal that the basic principles initiated within the society were greatly expanded through the internal structure of the class meeting. One such description, provided by Wesley, is recorded below:

> It can scarce be conceived what advantages have been reaped from this little prudential regulation [the class meeting]. Many now happily experience that Christian fellowship of which they had not so much as an idea before. They began to 'bear one another's

---

19. Watson, *The Early Methodists Class Meeting*, 94.
20. Watson, *The Early Methodists Class Meeting*, 105, 120.
21. Wesley, *The Works of John Wesley*, 8:257.

burdens,' and naturally to 'care for one another.' As they had daily a more intimate acquaintance with, so they had a more endeared affection for, each other. And speaking the truth in love, they grew up into him in all things, who is the head, even Christ, from whom the whole body, fitly joined together, and compacted by that which every joint supplied, according to the effectual working in the measure of every part, increased into the edifying of itself in love.[22]

Mutual accountability was inspired as each class member was prompted to "bear one another's burdens" and "care for one another" with a sincere heart. As each participant shared the progress or struggles related to their spiritual journey, the clear mandate to speak "the truth in love" commissioned class leaders "to advise, reprove, comfort, or exhort"[23] from the holy Scriptures, addressing the concerns of individual members with distinct biblical counsel.[24] Typical class meetings also enjoyed inspirational seasons of worship, warm fellowship, philanthropic outreach, and opportunities for group and individual prayer. Due to the fact that the class leader was appointed to facilitate both the sharing and instruction, only those of "sound judgment" and unmistakable devotion to Christ were selected for the post.[25]

Numerous outreach ministries were also initiated, funded, and staffed by class and society members. These ministries included orphanages, free medical assistance, regular visitation to the sick, a lending institution, schools for poor or abandoned children, a shelter to care for the blind, and a home for neglected widows.[26] In writing about the school for children, Wesley shared that "a happy change was soon observed in the children, both with regard to their tempers and behavior. They learned reading, writing, and arithmetic swiftly; and at the same time they were diligently instructed in the sound principles of religion, and earnestly exhorted to fear God and work out their own salvation."[27] To this end, the following commission furnished in the *General Rules* exhorted every believer to faithfully practice Christian service "by doing good, by being, in every kind, merciful after their power; as they have opportunity, doing good of

---

22. Wesley, *The Works of John Wesley*, 8:254.
23. Wesley, *The Works of John Wesley*, 8:270.
24. Watson, *The Early Methodists Class Meeting*, 96.
25. Wesley, *The Works of John Wesley*, 8:301.
26. Wesley, *The Letters of the Rev. John Wesley*, 2:306–10.
27. Wesley, *The Letters of the Rev. John Wesley*, 2:309.

every possible sort, and as far as is possible, to all men—to their bodies, of the ability which God giveth, by giving food to the hungry, by clothing the naked, by visiting or helping them that are sick, or in prison—to their souls, by instructing, reproving, or exhorting."[28] May the Holy God grant us both strength and determination so that we, through joyful obedience, might also fulfill these biblical mandates in our present day!

---

28. Wesley, *The Works of John Wesley*, 8:270–71.

7

Lessons

As stated in the introduction, the lessons of revival are important to master so, if by the gracious mercy of God, the reader experiences a season of spiritual awakening, they will be better equipped to cultivate its fruits. These lessons are also applicable to all who find themselves living in a dark season of history, longing for God to walk again among the nations, as they remind us of biblical mandates associated with individual and corporate renewal that are applicable for every day and age. Four concise lessons are provided below, and the reader is urged to prayerfully consider how God might desire to apply each lesson to their life and ministry.

Lesson 1

> The primary objective of revival is *not* the restoration of the church or the conversion of the lost. No! The ultimate objective of revival is to bring honor to the most holy One; for during such wondrous seasons our dear and sacred Savior, in all his perfection, is more purely worshiped, more supremely glorified, more wonderfully enjoyed, more deeply known, more reverently loved, and more vigorously obeyed by hearts subdued and concentrated for his service.

There is a sad tendency, of which I am guilty, to glory in the amazing stories of historic revival while neglecting the fundamental reason why such seasons were necessary. Seasons of historic genuine revival were necessary, as chapter one amply illustrated, because the church, the society, the family, the government, and the individual citizen had categorically offended the holy God by their thoughts, their words, and their deeds. His righteous name had been intolerably dishonored, his pure and holy word disregarded by incompetent or unconverted clergy, and the human family, created to glorify God and enjoy him forever, willfully and with abandon gave themselves to all manner of corruption.

Yet during the First Great Awakening the omnipotent God did what no man alone could accomplish; he restored the honor due to his great Name, and exalted the power of his holy word! Therefore, we study such seasons with both sadness and hope. Sadness that we, like our ancestors, persist in demeaning the name and the word of the most holy God. That we, like our ancestors, do not love God with our whole heart, mind, soul, or strength. Indeed, our churches, societies, governments, families, and individual lives have also willfully, and with blatant defiance, offended the supreme and most holy King! May we therefore earnestly, prayerfully, and with contrite hearts seek revival in our day and age so our dear and sacred Savior, in all his perfection, is more purely worshiped, more supremely glorified, more wonderfully enjoyed, more deeply known, more reverently loved, and more vigorously obeyed by hearts subdued and concentrated for his service.

Lesson 2

> Whereas revival is initiated and sustained supremely by God *at particular times in history*, renewal is viewed as the labor of an obedient believer or corporate community of faith *at any time in history*, initiated and sustained through the combination of spiritual disciplines and the power of the Holy Spirit. Renewal is the individual Christian and corporate community of faith joining in a singular "yes," resolving to both study and obey the whole counsel of God as revealed in the pages of sacred Scripture.

I would trust at this point in our study of the First Great Awakening the reader is convinced of the fact that genuine historic revival is initiated and sustained supremely by God. In the early eighteenth-century, when all social, political, and religious systems failed to produce any lasting transformation in the lives or hearts of the pitiful souls born during this era of decadence, the sovereign God issued the trumpet call of revival, and the nations in humble submission obeyed!

I am likewise hopeful that the study of the Great Awakening *society* and *class* convinced the reader that the spiritual disciplines represented in these eighteenth-century groups are generally applicable for biblical Christ-honoring believers in this present century as well. Any student of the Bible, for example, is aware that the Scriptures are replete with commands concerning the pursuit of personal holiness. Consider these words of Peter as an illustration, "As obedient children, do not be conformed to the passions of your former ignorance, but as he who called you is holy, you also be holy in all your conduct" (1 Pet 1:14–15 ESV). The first Psalm likewise declares the righteous are identified as those who habitually shun evil while meditating on the great law of God both "day and night." "Train yourself for godliness" are the instructions of Paul to his disciple Timothy (1 Tim 4:7 ESV). "But seek first the kingdom of God and his righteousness" decrees our Lord (Matt 6:33). Indeed, all who belong to Christ should be found working out their "own salvation with fear and trembling," fully relying on the One who empowers them "both to will and to work for his good pleasure" (Phil 2:12–13 ESV).

The general structures of the *society* and *class* furnish an ideal illustration of the practical application of these biblical mandates within the context of a faith community. For example, the reader may recall the *General Rules* of the *society* required its membership to "continue to evidence their desire of salvation . . . by attending upon all the ordinances of God. Such are, the public worship of God, the ministry of the word, either read or expounded, the Supper of the Lord, family and private prayer, searching the Scriptures, and fasting, or abstinence."[1] Mutual accountability was likewise inspired in the *class* structure as each member was prompted to "bear one another's burdens" and "care for one another." As each participant shared the progress or struggles related to their spiritual journey, the clear mandate to speak "the truth in love" commissioned class leaders "to advise, reprove, comfort, or exhort"[2] from the holy Scriptures, addressing the concerns of individual members with distinct biblical counsel.[3]

Numerous outreach ministries initiated, funded, and staffed by *class* and *society* members fulfilled the Lord's decree to "love your neighbor as yourself" (Mk 12:31 ESV). These ministries included orphanages, free medical assistance, regular visitation to the sick, a lending institution, schools for poor or abandoned children, a shelter to care for the blind and a home for neglected widows.[4] In similar fashion the following commission furnished in the *General Rules* exhorted every believer to faithfully practice Christian service "by doing good, by being, in every kind, merciful after

---

1. Wesley, *The Works of John Wesley*, 8:271.
2. Wesley, *The Works of John Wesley*, 8:270.
3. Watson, *The Early Methodists Class Meeting*, 96.
4. Wesley, *The Letters of the Rev. John Wesley*, 2:306–10.

their power; as they have opportunity, doing good of every possible sort, and as far as is possible, to all men—to their bodies, of the ability which God giveth, by giving food to the hungry, by clothing the naked, by visiting or helping them that are sick, or in prison—to their souls, by instructing, reproving, or exhorting."[5]

Do the descriptions of the biblical conduct practiced by *class* and *society* members mirror your life, your small group, your Sunday school class, or the general membership of your local church? Most of us, with deep lament, would likely mourn the absence of such biblical Christianity in our lives and corporate communities of faith. What can we do? We must begin with ourselves, and our immediate sphere of influence. With earnest intent we can resolve to cultivate a deeper devotion to Christ through spiritual disciplines that foster personal holiness. We can determine to study and obey the whole counsel of God, the sacred Scriptures, depending upon the Holy Spirit for conviction, wisdom, insight, and power. We can give evidence of our salvation "by attending upon all the ordinances of God. Such are, the public worship of God, the ministry of the word, either read or expounded, the supper of the Lord, family and private prayer, searching the Scriptures, and fasting, or abstinence."[6] We can call a few of our believing friends and resolve, with the help of God, to "bear one another's burdens" and "care for one another."[7] We can more intentionally love our neighbor "by doing good of every possible sort, and as far as is possible, to all men."[8]

The corporate church, the body of Christ, is comprised of its individual members. A strong Christ-honoring biblical church is thus a collective gathering of individual, biblically sound, Christ-honoring believers. In light of these truths, I would exhort you to recall that the company of the Lamb is comprised of resolute men and women who are committed to cultivating a deeper devotion to Christ through spiritual disciplines that foster personal holiness; determined to both study and obey the sacred Scriptures, depending upon the Holy Spirit for conviction, wisdom, insight, and power. Will you, will I, be counted among the resolute and consecrated company of biblical Christ-honoring believers?

---

5. Wesley, *The Works of John Wesley*, 8:270–71.
6. Wesley, *The Works of John Wesley*, 8:271.
7. Wesley, *The Works of John Wesley*, 8:270.
8. Wesley, *The Works of John Wesley*, 8:270–71.

Lesson 3

The sermons preached by the clergy who were used mightily by God throughout the First Great Awakening were, with a few exceptions, biblically-centered and doctrinally sound.

What era in the history of the Christian do you believe historian Henry Fish was describing when he stated, "the vast majority of sermons were miserable moral essays, utterly devoid of anything calculated to awaken, convert, sanctify, or save souls?"[9] The astute reader may recall this quotation from chapter one where Fish was recounting the substance of the typical sermon preached from European pulpits in the early eighteenth-century. With all due respect to contemporary clergy, a group to which I belong, the question needs to be asked if the sermons or teachings presented in a majority of the present-day Christian churches resemble, at least to some degree, the description rendered by Fish?

As you further reflect on the previous question, you may wish to compare Fish's appraisal of the eighteenth-century pulpit with the four Great Awakening sermons catalogued in Appendix one and two. Consider, by means of illustration, the message by William Tennent titled, *An Exhortation to Walk in Christ*. Observe how biblically-centered and doctrinally sound were his words; all but the coldest of hearts should be awakened, moved, rebuked, challenged, and drawn to Christ as they meditate on his message! The research, study, and writing of such messages must have been a monumental task for these men whose scholastic resources were limited and days interrupted by common ministerial duties. These Great Awakening pulpiteers clearly held the biblical mandate high, as they were reminded of the King's command to present themselves "to God as one approved, a worker who has no need to be ashamed, rightly handling the word of truth" (2 Tim 2:15 ESV). They also evidently labored to fulfill the following instruction Paul provided to his protégé, Timothy, to "preach the word; be ready in season and out of season; reprove, rebuke, and exhort, with complete patience and teaching" (2 Tim 4:2 ESV). Are there biblically-centered and doctrinally sound clergy in our day? Would your name, would mine, be found among them? Might these biblical exhortations prove to be true in the ministries of an increasing number of Christian pastors or teachers who have likewise been entrusted with the sacred ministry of the word!

---

9. Fish, *Handbook of Revivals*, 45.

Lesson 4

When biblically orthodox pastors are united on primary theological truths, they should consider laboring together, to the degree their Spirit-directed conscience allows, to advance the kingdom.

As a pastor who embraces a Reformed theological perspective, I present this fourth and final lesson thoughtfully. I will borrow insights from the prefatory notes for Appendix One to help frame my comments. In the prefatory notes I advocate my firmly held conviction that pastors should be theologically grounded and preach clear doctrinal truth. In addition, I suggest most theological or doctrinal conflict *is resolvable*. As an illustration, I propose that either the Calvinist (Reformed) perspective on election and final perseverance is biblically true, or the Arminian perspective is biblically true. It is theologically dishonest to declare the Scripture allows for both perspectives to be equally true! In this regard my challenge to the reader, and continually to myself as well, is to ensure we are theologically biblical to our core, seeking through ardent interpretative study to understand what the Scriptures clearly present as doctrinal truth.

In the prefatory notes I also ponder the divine and sovereign decision of the omniscient God in appointing Whitefield, the devoted Calvinist, and Wesley, the convinced Arminian, to be his principal vessels in the First Great Awakening. Upon reflection of God's faultless design, I suggested the sovereign calling of Whitefield and Wesley could lead us to conclude that biblically orthodox pastors, who are united on primary theological truths, should consider laboring together to advance the kingdom. The difficulty at this juncture comes in defining *primary theological truths*. In response to this comment, I suggested the following were among the *primary theological truths* advocated by both Wesley and Whitefield—Both evangelists acknowledged that apart from Christ, one was totally lost and without hope. Both affirmed the necessity of a new birth. Both believed in a literal heaven and a literal hell. Both articulated clearly the great truth that justification was by faith, and faith alone. Both held the Bible to be the sole authority for life and living, and nothing less than the absolute inspired and inherent word of God. Both were Trinitarians, and both practiced a bold proclamation of the gospel, mercy ministry, missions, and the pursuit of holiness. Perhaps their common assent to the basic tenets of the Nicene Creed should be added to the above list, as this historic document provides insight on other primary areas of doctrinal compatibility.

As I provide concluding thoughts to this particular lesson, I recognize that the application of this principle will be somewhat subjective. In other words, biblically orthodox pastors who are united *on primary theological truths* should consider laboring together to advance the kingdom. Each pastor will therefore need to determine which theological and doctrinal truths they consider to be *primary*, as well as to what *degree their Spirit-directed conscience allows them* to labor alongside others of differing theological perspectives to advance common kingdom goals. May God therefore grant us wisdom to know to what degree we can serve alongside others—others who are genuinely converted and joined with us in the one body of Christ, expending our lives together for the honor of the King, and the advancement of his kingdom.

APPENDIX 1

Sermons by George Whitefield and John Wesley

Prefatory Notes

THE SERMONS OF WHITEFIELD and Wesley contain doctrinal teaching, inspirational encouragement, evangelistic appeals, and are readily accessible today. The names Whitefield and Wesley are likewise well-known within many Protestant theological circles. Perhaps not as widely known is the fact that during the early years of the Great Awakening the relationship between these two men was considerably strained. Most historians would agree that the primary area of contention was theological, focusing particularly on the doctrines of election and final perseverance. Whitefield held a Reformed view of election and final perseverance, whereas Wesley espoused the Armenian perspective.

Early correspondence by Wesley provides an indication that he and his colleague Whitefield had determined not to allow their theological differences to be a cause for division. To this end Wesley, in April 1739, writes the following reflections to a trusted colleague, "Our dear brethren, before I left London, and our brother Whitefield here, and our brother Chapman since, had conjured me to enter into no disputes, least of all concerning predestination, because this people was to deeply prejudiced for it. The same was my own inclination."[1]

After Whitefield left for America in August of that same year Wesley's thoughts were changed through the casting of lots. He determined it was prudent to make his theological differences with Whitefield known to the wider populace; first through preaching, and later through publishing a controversial sermon titled *Free Grace*. Briefly stated, the primary objective

---

1. Wesley, *The Letters of the Rev. John Wesley*, 1:302.

of the published sermon was to denounce the Calvinistic perspective on predestination and advance the Arminian viewpoint. This document inflamed the existing tension between Whitefield and Wesley, along with many of their loyal followers. A flurry of correspondence between the two ensued, a sample of which is noted below. The first comments are from the pen of Whitefield, and the second from writings of Wesley.

> I beseech you, by the mercies of God in Christ Jesus our Lord, if you would have my love confirmed towards you, write no more to me about misrepresentation wherein we differ.... If possible, I am ten thousand times more convinced of the doctrine of *election*, and the *final perseverance* of those that are truly in Christ, than when I saw you last. You think otherwise. Why then should we dispute, when there is no probability of convincing?[2]

> The case is quite plain. There are bigots both for predestination and against it. God is sending a message to those on either side. But neither will receive it, unless from one who is of their own opinion. Therefore, for a time, you are suffered to be of one opinion, and I of another. But when his time is come, God will do what man cannot, namely, make us both of one mind.[3]

Whitefield wrote a retort to Wesley's *Free Grace* message in December of 1740, but delayed its publication until March of 1741 as he was perhaps hoping to avoid further disputes with his comrade. Sadly, the journals of both men indicate that the entire year of 1740, and a good portion of 1741, was spent in discord. Various correspondences between the two indicate there was a measure of reconciliation in the spring of 1742, which continued in differing degrees throughout their lifetimes. In terms of their opposing doctrinal views, neither renounced their convictions.

Why this brief synopsis of a seemingly unresolvable theological conflict in the midst of what was arguably one of the finest eras of Christian history? Hopefully, so we can learn its lessons! The lessons I would like to propose are two, the first of which is to suggest that most theological conflict *is resolvable*! By this statement I mean that an in-depth theological study of the doctrines of election and final perseverance, for example, will reveal the truth that one theological interpretative system is correct, and the other is not. In other words, either the Reformed or Calvinistic understanding of election and final perseverance is biblically true, or the

2. Tyerman, *The Life of The Rev John Wesley*, 1:313–314.
3. Tyerman, *The Life of The Rev John Wesley*, 1:315–316.

Arminian perspective of these two doctrines is biblically true. In this regard all who seek to be true biblical pastors and teachers should study these and other difficult doctrines thoroughly to ensure their understanding corresponds to a theologically accurate interpretation of the Bible.

The second lesson centers on the mystery and wonder of the sovereign God appointing Whitefield and Wesley to be his principal vessels in the First Great Awakening. What can be learned from the divine selection of two such different men? The divine calling of Whitefield and Wesley may suggest that biblically orthodox pastors, who are united *on primary theological truths* should consider laboring together, *to the degree their Spirit-directed conscience allows them*, to advance the kingdom. What primary theological truths were common to Whitefield and Wesley? Both evangelists acknowledged that apart from Christ, one was totally lost and without hope. Both affirmed the necessity of a new birth. Both believed in a literal heaven and a literal hell. Both articulated clearly the great truth that justification was by faith, and faith alone. Both held the Bible to be the sole authority for life and living, and nothing less than the absolute inspired and inherent word of God. Both were Trinitarians, and both practiced a bold proclamation of the gospel, mercy ministry, missions, and the pursuit of holiness. Both agreed that one could find no greater joy than spending their lives for the work of Christ, and both did just that.

The fine sermons contained in this appendix, although furnishing hints to their particular and distinctive persuasions, are poignant illustrations of the fact that these two evangelists agreed on numerous doctrines that are central to Christian faith and practice. Might we likewise give emphasis to the proclamation of the conservative orthodox Christian doctrines that are primary, while attending to the more divisive issues through prudent theological study and discussion, seasoned by large measures of charity.

APPENDIX 1: SERMONS BY GEORGE WHITEFIELD AND JOHN WESLEY

Sermon by George Whitefield—*The Method of Grace*

Jeremiah 6:14, "They have healed also the hurt of the daughter of my people slightly, saying, Peace, peace, when there is no peace."

As God can send a nation or people no greater blessing than to give them faithful, sincere, and upright ministers, so the greatest curse that God can possibly send upon a people in this world is to give them over to blind, unregenerate, carnal, lukewarm, and unskilled guides. And yet, in all ages, we find that there have been many wolves in sheep's clothing; many that daubed with untempered mortar, that prophesied smoother things than God did allow. As it was formerly, so it is now; there are many that corrupt the word of God and deal deceitfully with it. It was so in a special manner in the Prophet Jeremiah's time; and he, faithful to his Lord, faithful to that God who employed him, did not fail from time to time to open his mouth against them, and to bear a noble testimony to the honor of that God in whose name he from time to time spake.

If you will read this prophecy, you will find that none spake more against such ministers than Jeremiah, and here especially in the chapter out of which the text is taken, he speaks very severely against them—he charges them with several crimes; particularly, he charges them with covetousness, "For," says he in the 13th verse, "from the least of them even to the greatest of them, everyone is given to covetousness; and from the prophet even unto the priest, everyone dealeth false." And then, in the words of the text, in a more special manner, he exemplifies how they had dealt falsely, how they had behaved treacherously to poor souls. Says he, "They have healed also the hurt of the daughter of my people slightly, saying, Peace, peace, when there is no peace."

The Prophet, in the name of God, had been denouncing war against the people, he had been telling them that their house should be left desolate, and that the Lord would certainly visit the land with war. "Therefore," says he in the 11th verse, "I am full of the fury of the Lord; I am weary with holding in; I will pour it out upon the children abroad, and upon the assembly of young men together; for even the husband with the wife shall be taken, the aged with him that is full of days. And their houses shall be turned unto others, with their fields and wives together; for I will stretch out my hand upon the inhabitants of the land, saith the Lord." The Prophet gives a thundering message, that they might be terrified and have some convictions and inclinations to repent; but it seems that the false prophets, the false priests, went about stifling people's convictions, and when they were hurt or a little terrified, they were for daubing over the wound, telling them that Jeremiah was but an enthusiastic preacher, that there could be no such thing as war among them, and saying to people, Peace, peace, be still, when the Prophet told them there was no peace.

The words, then, refer primarily unto outward things; but I verily believe have also a further reference to the soul, and are to be referred to those false teachers who, when people were under conviction of sin, when people were beginning to look towards heaven, were for stifling their convictions and telling them they were good enough before. And, indeed, people generally love to have it so; our hearts are exceedingly deceitful, and desperately wicked; none but the eternal God knows how treacherous they are. How many of us cry, Peace, peace, to our souls, when there is no peace! How many are there who are now settled upon their lees, that now think they are Christians, that now flatter themselves that they have an interest in Jesus Christ; whereas if we come to examine their experiences, we shall find that their peace is but a peace of the devil's making—it is not a peace of God's giving—it is not a peace that passeth human understanding. It is a matter, therefore, of great importance my dear hearers, to know whether we may speak peace to our hearts. We are all desirous of peace; peace is an unspeakable blessing; how can we live without peace? And, therefore, people from time to time must be taught how far they must go, and what must be wrought in them, before they can speak peace to their hearts.

First, then, before you can speak peace to your hearts you must be made to see, made to feel, made to weep over, made to bewail your actual transgressions against the law of God. According to the covenant of works, "The soul that sinneth it shall die"; cursed is that man, be he what he may, that continueth not in all things that are written in the book of the Law to do them. We are not only to do some things, but we are to do all things, and we are to continue so to do; so that the least deviation from the moral law, according to the covenant of works, whether in thought, word, or deed, deserves eternal death at the hand of God. And if one evil thought, if one evil word, if one evil action, deserves eternal damnation, how many hells, my friends, do every one of us deserve, whose whole lives have been one continued rebellion against God! Before ever, therefore, you can speak peace to your hearts, you must be brought to see, brought to believe, what a dreadful thing it is to depart from the living God.

And now, my dear friends, examine your hearts, for I hope you came hither with a design to have your souls made better. Give me leave to ask you, in the presence of God, whether you know the time, and if you do not know exactly the time, do you know there was a time when God wrote bitter things against you, when the arrows of the Almighty were within you? Was ever the remembrance of your sins grievous to you? Was the burden of your sins intolerable to your thoughts? Did you ever see that God's wrath might justly fall upon you, on account of your actual transgressions against God? Were you ever in all your life sorry for your sins? Could you ever say, my sins are gone over my head as a burden too heavy for me to bear? Did you ever experience any such thing as this? Did ever any such thing as this pass between God and your soul? If not, for Jesus Christ's sake, do not call yourselves Christians; you may speak peace to your hearts, but there is no peace. May the Lord awaken you, may the Lord convert you, may the Lord give you peace, if it be his will, before you go home!

But further, you may be convinced of your actual sins, so as to be made to tremble, and yet you may be strangers to Jesus Christ; you may have no true work of grace upon your hearts. Before ever, therefore, you can speak peace to your hearts, conviction must go deeper; you must not only be convinced of your actual transgressions against the law of God, but likewise of the foundation of all your transgressions. And what is that? I mean original sin, that original corruption each of us brings into the world with us, which renders us liable to God's wrath and damnation. There are many poor souls that think themselves fine reasoners, yet they pretend to say there is no such thing as original sin; they will charge God with injustice in imputing Adam's sin to us; although we have got the mark of the beast and of the devil upon us, yet they tell us we are not born in sin. Let them look abroad into the world and see the disorders in it, and think, if they can, if this is the paradise in which God did put man. No! Everything in the world is out of order.

If we look inwardly, we shall see enough of lusts, and man's temper contrary to the temper of God. There is pride, malice, and revenge in all our hearts; and this temper cannot come from God, it comes from our first parent, Adam, who, after he fell from God, fell out of God into the devil. However, therefore, some people may deny this; yet when conviction comes, all carnal reasoning's are battered down immediately, and the poor soul begins to feel and see the fountain from which all the polluted streams do flow.

APPENDIX 1: SERMONS BY GEORGE WHITEFIELD AND JOHN WESLEY

When the sinner is first awakened, he begins to wonder—How came I to be so wicked? The Spirit of God then strikes in, and shows that he has no good thing in him by nature; then he sees that he is altogether gone out of the way, that he is altogether become abominable, and the poor creature is made to lie down at the foot of the throne of God and to acknowledge that God would be just to damn him, just to cut him off, though he never had committed one actual sin in his life. Did you ever feel and experience this, any of you—to justify God in your damnation—to own that you are by nature children of wrath, and that God may justly cut you off, though you never actually had offended him in all your life? If you were ever truly convicted, if your hearts were ever truly cut, if self were truly taken out of you, you would be made to see and feel this. And if you have never felt the weight of original sin, do not call yourselves Christians.

I am verily persuaded original sin is the greatest burden of a true convert; this ever grieves the regenerate soul, the sanctified soul. The indwelling of sin in the heart is the burden of a converted person; it is the burden of a true Christian. He continually cries out, "O! who will deliver me from this body of death," this indwelling corruption in my heart? This is that which disturbs a poor soul most. And, therefore, if you never felt this inward corruption, if you never saw that God might justly curse you for it, indeed, my dear friends, you may speak peace to your hearts, but I fear, nay, I know, there is no true peace.

Further, before you can speak peace to your hearts, you must not only be troubled for the sins of your life, the sin of your nature, but likewise for the sins of your best duties and performances. When a poor soul is somewhat awakened by the terrors of the Lord, then the poor creature, being born under the covenant of works, flies directly to a covenant of works again. And as Adam and Eve hid themselves among the trees of the garden, and sewed fig leaves together to cover their nakedness, so the poor sinner, when awakened, flies to his duties and to his performances, to hide himself from God, and goes to patch up a righteousness of his own. Says he, I will be mighty good now—I will reform—I will do all I can; and then certainly Jesus Christ will have mercy on me. But before you can speak peace to your heart, you must be brought to see that God may damn you for the best prayer you ever put up; you must be brought to see that all your duties—all your righteousness—as the Prophet elegantly expresses it—put them all together, are so far from recommending you to God, are so far from being any motive and inducement to God to have mercy on your poor soul, that he will see them to be filthy rags, a menstruous cloth—that God hates them, and cannot away with them, if you bring them to him in order to recommend you to his favor.

My dear friends, what is there in our performances to recommend us unto God? Our persons are in an unjustified state by nature, we deserve to be damned ten thousand times over, and what must our performances be? We can do no good thing by nature, "They that are in the flesh cannot please God." You may do many things materially good, but you cannot do a thing formally and rightly good; because nature cannot act above itself. It is impossible that a man who is unconverted can act for the glory of God; he cannot do anything in faith, and "whatsoever is not of faith is sin."

After we are renewed, yet we are renewed but in part; indwelling sin continues in us, there is a mixture of corruption in every one of our duties; so that after we are converted, were Jesus Christ only to accept us according to our works, our works would damn us, for we cannot put up a prayer but it is far from that perfection which the moral law requireth. I do not know what you may think, but I can say that I cannot pray but I sin—I cannot preach to you or any others but I sin—I can do nothing without sin; and, as one expresseth it, my repentance wants to be repented of, and my tears to be washed in the precious blood of my dear Redeemer. Our best duties are as so many splendid sins. Before you can speak peace in your heart, you must not only be made sick of your original and actual sin, but you must be made sick of your righteousness, of all your duties and performances. There must be a deep conviction before you can be brought out of your self-righteousness; it is the last idol taken out of our heart. The pride of our heart will not let us submit to the righteousness of Jesus Christ. But if you never felt that you had a righteousness of your own, if you never felt the deficiency of your own righteousness, you cannot come to Jesus Christ.

There are a great many now who may say, well, we believe all this, but there is a great difference betwixt talking and feeling. Did you ever feel the want of a dear Redeemer? Did you ever feel the want of Jesus Christ, upon the account of the deficiency of your own righteousness? And can you now say from your heart, Lord, thou mayst justly damn me for the best duties that ever I did perform? If you are not thus brought out of self, you may speak peace to yourselves, but yet there is no peace.

But then, before you can speak peace to your souls, there is one particular sin you must be greatly troubled for, and yet I fear there are few of you think what it is; it is the reigning, the damning sin of the Christian world, and yet the Christian world seldom or never think of it. And pray what is that? It is what most of you think you are not guilty of—and that is, the sin of unbelief. Before you can speak peace to your heart, you must be troubled for the unbelief of your heart. But, can it be supposed that any of you are unbelievers here in this church-yard, that are born in Scotland, in a reformed country, that go to church every Sabbath? Can any of you that receive the sacrament once a year—O that it were administered oftener!—can it be supposed that you who had tokens for the sacrament, that you who keep up family prayer, that any of you do not believe in the Lord Jesus Christ? I appeal to your own hearts, if you would not think me uncharitable, if I doubted whether any of you believed in Christ; and yet, I fear upon examination, we should find that most of you have not so much faith in the Lord Jesus Christ as the devil himself.

I am persuaded the devil believes more of the Bible than most of us do. He believes the divinity of Jesus Christ; that is more than many who call themselves Christians do; nay, he believes and trembles, and that is more than thousands amongst us do. My friends, we mistake a historical faith for a true faith, wrought in the heart by the Spirit of God. You fancy you believe, because you believe there is such a book as we call the Bible—because you go to church; all this you may do, and have no true faith in Christ. Merely to believe there was such a person as Christ, merely to believe there is a book called the Bible, will do you no good, more than to believe there was such a man as Caesar or Alexander the Great.

My dear friends, I am more particular in this, because it is a most deceitful delusion, whereby so many people are carried away, that they believe already. Therefore, it is remarked of Mr. Marshall, giving account of his experiences, that he had been working for life, and he had arranged all his sins under the ten commandments, and then coming to a minister, asked him the reason why he could not get peace. The minister looked at his catalogue; Away, says he, I do not find one word of the sin of unbelief in all your catalogue. It is the peculiar work of the Spirit of God to convince us of our unbelief—that we have got no faith. Says Jesus Christ, "I will send the Comforter; and when he is come, he will reprove the world" of the sin of unbelief; "of sin," says Christ, "because they believe not on me."

Now, my dear friends, did God ever show you that you had no faith? Were you ever made to bewail a hard heart of unbelief? Was it ever the language of your heart, Lord, give me faith; Lord, enable me to lay hold on thee; Lord, enable me to call thee *my* Lord and *my* God? Did Jesus Christ ever convince you in this manner? Did he ever convince you of your inability to close with Christ, and make you to cry out to God to give you faith? If not, do not speak peace to your heart. May the Lord awaken you, and give you true, solid peace before you go hence and be no more!

Once more then, before you can speak peace to your heart, you must not only be convinced of your actual and original sin, the sins of your own righteousness, the sin of unbelief, but you must be enabled to lay hold upon the perfect righteousness, the all-sufficient righteousness, of the Lord Jesus Christ; you must lay hold by faith on the righteousness of Jesus Christ, and then you shall have peace. "Come," says Jesus, "unto me, all ye that are weary and heavy laden, and I will give you rest." This speaks encouragement to all that are weary and heavy laden; but the promise of rest is made to them only upon their coming, and believing, and taking him to be their God and their all.

Before we can ever have peace with God, we must be justified by faith through our Lord Jesus Christ, we must be enabled to apply Christ to our hearts, we must have Christ brought home to our souls, so as his righteousness may be made our righteousness, so as his merits may be imputed to our souls. My dear friends, were you ever married to Jesus Christ? Did Jesus Christ ever give himself to you? Did you ever close with Christ by a lively faith, so as to feel Christ in your hearts, so as to hear him speaking peace to your souls? Did peace ever flow in upon your hearts like a river? Did you ever feel that peace that Christ spoke to his disciples? I pray God he may come and speak peace to you.

Give me leave, then, to address myself to several sorts of persons; and O may God, of his infinite mercy, bless the application! There are some of you perhaps can say, through grace we can go along with you. Blessed be God, we have been convinced of our actual sins, we have been convinced of original sin, we have been convinced of self-righteousness, we have felt the bitterness of unbelief, and through grace we have closed with Jesus Christ; we can speak peace to our hearts, because God hath spoken peace to us. Can you say so? Then I will salute you, as the angels did the women the first day of the week, All hail! Fear not ye, my dear brethren, you are happy souls; you may lie down and be at peace indeed, for God hath given you peace; you may be content under all the dispensations of providence, for nothing can happen to you now, but what shall be the effect of God's love to your soul; you need not fear what sightings may be without, seeing there is peace within. Have you closed with Christ? Is God your friend?

Is Christ your friend? Then, look up with comfort; all is yours, and you are Christ's, and Christ is God's. Everything shall work together for your good; the very hairs of your head are numbered; he that toucheth you, toucheth the apple of God's eye.

But then, my dear friends, beware of resting on your first conversion. You that are young believers in Christ, you should be looking out for fresh discoveries of the Lord Jesus Christ every moment; you must not build upon your past experiences, you must not build upon a work within you, but always come out of yourselves to the righteousness of Jesus Christ without you; you must be always coming as poor sinners to draw water out of the wells of salvation; you must be forgetting the things that are behind, and be continually pressing forward to the things that are before. My dear friends, you must keep up a tender, close walk with the Lord Jesus Christ.

There are many of us who lose our peace by our untender walk; something or other gets in betwixt Christ and us, and we fall into darkness; something or other steals our hearts from God, and this grieves the Holy Ghost, and the Holy Ghost leaves us to ourselves. Let me, therefore, exhort you that have got peace with God, to take care that you do not lose this peace. It is true, if you are once in Christ, you cannot finally fall from God, "There is no condemnation to them that are in Christ Jesus"; but if you cannot fall finally, you may fall foully, and may go with broken bones all your days. Take care of backslidings; for Jesus Christ's sake, do not grieve the Holy Ghost—you may never recover your comfort while you live. O take care of going a gadding and wandering from God, after you have closed with Jesus Christ. My dear friends, I have paid dear for backsliding. Our hearts are so cursedly wicked that if you take not care, if you do not keep up a constant watch, your wicked hearts will deceive you, and draw you aside. It will be sad to be under the scourge of a correcting Father; witness the visitation of Job, David, and other saints in Scripture. Let me, therefore, exhort you that have got peace to keep a close walk with Christ.

I am grieved with the loose walk of those that are Christians, that have had discoveries of Jesus Christ; there is so little difference betwixt them and other people, that I scarce know which is the true Christian. Christians are afraid to speak of God—they run down with the stream; if they come into worldly company, they will talk of the world as if they were in their element; this you would not do when you had the first discoveries of Christ's love; you could talk then of Christ's love for ever, when the candle of the Lord shined upon your soul. That time has been when you had something to say for your dear Lord; but now you can go into company and hear others speaking about the world bold enough, and you are afraid of being laughed at if you speak for Jesus Christ. A great many people have grown conformists now in the worst sense of the word; they will cry out against the ceremonies of the church, as they may justly do; but then you are mighty fond of ceremonies in your behavior, you will conform to the world, which is a great deal worse. Many will stay till the devil bring up new fashions. Take care, then, not to be conformed to the world.

What have Christians to do with the world? Christians should be singularly good, bold for their Lord, that all who are with you may take notice that you have been with Jesus. I would exhort you to come to a settlement in Jesus Christ, so as to have a continual abiding of God in your heart. We go a-building on our faith of adherence and lost our comfort; but we should be growing up to a faith of assurance, to know that we are God's, and so walk in the comfort of the Holy Ghost and be edified.

Jesus Christ is now much wounded in the house of his friends. Excuse me in being particular; for, my friends, it grieves me more that Jesus Christ should be wounded by his friends than by his enemies. We cannot expect anything else from Deists; but for such as have felt his power, to fall away, for them not to walk agreeably to the vocation wherewith they are called—by these means we bring our Lord's religion into contempt, to be a byword among the heathen. For Christ's sake, if you know Christ keep close by him; if God have spoken peace, O keep that peace by looking up to Jesus Christ every moment. Such as have got peace with God, if you are under trials, fear not, all things shall work for your good; if you are under temptations, fear not, if he has spoken peace to your hearts, all these things shall be for your good.

But what shall I say to you that have got no peace with God?—and these are, perhaps, the most of this congregation; it makes me weep to think of it. Most of you, if you examine your hearts, must confess that God never yet spoke peace to you; you are children of the devil, if Christ is not in you, if God has not spoken peace to your heart. Poor soul! What a cursed condition are you in. I would not be in your case for ten thousand, thousand worlds. Why? You are just hanging over hell. What peace can you have when God is your enemy, when the wrath of God is abiding upon your poor soul?

Awake, then, you that are sleeping in a false peace; awake, ye carnal professors, ye hypocrites that go to church, receive the sacrament, read your Bibles, and never felt the power of God upon your hearts; you that are formal professors, you that are baptized heathens; awake, awake, and do not rest on a false bottom. Blame me not for addressing myself to you; indeed, it is out of love to your souls. I see you are lingering in your Sodom and wanting to stay there; but I come to you as the angel did to Lot, to take you by the hand. Come away, my dear brethren—fly, fly, fly for your lives to Jesus Christ, fly to a bleeding God, fly to a throne of grace; and beg of God to break your hearts, beg of God to convince you of your actual sins, beg of God to convince you of your original sin, beg of God to convince you of your self-righteousness—beg of God to give you faith, and to enable you to close with Jesus Christ.

O you that are secure, I must be a son of thunder to you, and O that God may awaken you, though it be with thunder; it is out of love, indeed, that I speak to you. I know by sad experience what it is to be lulled asleep with a false peace; long was I lulled asleep, long did I think myself a Christian, when I knew nothing of the Lord Jesus Christ. I went perhaps farther than many of you do; I used to fast twice a week, I used to pray sometimes nine times a day, I used to receive the sacrament constantly every Lord's day; and yet I knew nothing of Jesus Christ in my heart, I knew not that I must be a new creature—I knew nothing of inward religion in my soul. And perhaps many of you may be deceived as I, poor creature, was; and therefore, it is out of love to you indeed, that I speak to you.

O if you do not take care, a form of religion will destroy your soul; you will rest in it and will not come to Jesus Christ at all; whereas, these things are only the means, and not the end of religion; Christ is the end of the law for righteousness to all that believe. O, then, awake, you that are settled on your lees; awake you church professors; awake you that have got a name to live, that are rich and think you want nothing, not considering that you are poor, and blind, and naked; I counsel you to come and buy of Jesus Christ gold, white raiment, and eye-salve. But I hope there are some that are a little wounded; I hope God does not intend to let me preach in vain; I hope God will reach some of your precious souls, and awaken some of you out of your carnal security; I hope there are some who are willing to come to Christ, and beginning to think that they have been building upon a false foundation.

Perhaps the devil may strike in, and bid you despair of mercy; but fear not, what I have been speaking to you is only out of love to you—is only to awaken you, and let you see your danger. If any of you are willing to be reconciled to God, God the Father, Son, and Holy Ghost, is willing to be reconciled to you. O then, though you have no peace as yet, come away to Jesus Christ; he is our peace, he is our peace-maker—he has made peace betwixt God and offending man. Would you have peace with God? Away then, to God through Jesus Christ, who has purchased peace; the Lord Jesus has shed his heart's blood for this. He died for this; he rose again for this; he ascended into the highest heaven and is now interceding at the right hand of God.

Perhaps you think there will be no peace for you. Why so? Because you are sinners? Because you have crucified Christ—you have put him to open shame—you have trampled underfoot the blood of the Son of God? What of all this? Yet there is peace for you. Pray, what did Jesus Christ say of his disciples, when he came to them the first day of the week? The first word he said was, "Peace be unto you"; he showed them his hands, and his side, and said, "Peace be unto you." It is as much as if he had said, fear not, my disciples; see my hands and my feet how they have been pierced for your sake; therefore, fear not.

How did Christ speak to his disciples? Go tell my brethren, and tell broken-hearted Peter in particular, that Christ is risen, that he is ascended unto his Father and your Father, to his God and your God. And after Christ rose from the dead, he came preaching peace, with an olive branch of peace, like Noah's dove, "My peace I leave with you." Who were they? They were enemies of Christ as well as we, they were deniers of Christ once as well as we. Perhaps some of you have backslidden and lost your peace, and you think you deserve no peace; and no more you do. But, then, God will heal your backslidings, he will love you freely. As for you that are wounded, if you are made willing to come to Christ, come away.

Perhaps some of you want to dress yourselves in your duties, that are but rotten rags. No, you had better come naked as you are, for you must throw aside your rags, and come in your blood. Some of you may say we would come, but we have got a hard heart. But you will never get it made soft till ye come to Christ; he will take away the heart of stone and give you a heart of flesh; he will speak peace to your souls; though ye have betrayed him, yet he will be your peace. Shall I prevail upon any of you this morning to come to Jesus Christ? There is a great multitude of souls here; how shortly must you all die and go to judgment! Even before night, or to-morrow's night, some of you may be laid out for this kirk-yard. And how will you do if you be not at peace with God—if the Lord Jesus Christ has not spoken peace to your heart? If God speak not peace to you here, you will be damned forever.

I must not flatter you, my dear friends; I will deal sincerely with your souls. Some of you may think I carry things too far. But, indeed, when you come to judgment, you will find what I say is true, either to your eternal damnation or comfort. May God influence your hearts to come to him! I am not willing to go away without persuading you. I cannot be persuaded but God may make use of me as a means of persuading some of you to come to the Lord Jesus Christ. O did you but feel the peace which they have that love the Lord Jesus Christ! "Great peace have they," say the Psalmist, "that love thy law; nothing shall offend them." But there is no peace to the wicked.

I know what it is to live a life of sin; I was obliged to sin in order to stifle conviction. And I am sure this is the way many of you take; if you get into company, you drive off conviction. But you had better go to the bottom at once; it must be done—your wound must be searched, or you must be damned. If it were a matter of indifference, I would not speak one word about it. But you will be damned without Christ. He is the way, he is the truth, and the life. I cannot think you should go to hell without Christ. How can you dwell with everlasting burnings? How can you abide the thought of living with the devil forever? Is it not better to have some soul-trouble here, then to be sent to hell by Jesus Christ hereafter? What is hell, but to be absent from Christ? If there were no other hell, that would be hell enough. It will be hell to be tormented with the devil forever.

Get acquaintance with God, then, and be at peace. I beseech you, as a poor worthless ambassador of Jesus Christ, that you would be reconciled to God. My business this morning, the first day of the week, is to tell you that Christ is willing to be reconciled to you. Will any of you be reconciled to Jesus Christ? Then, he will forgive you all your sins, he will blot out all your transgressions. But if you will go on and rebel against Christ and stab him daily—if you will go on and abuse Jesus Christ, the wrath of God you must expect will fall upon you. God will not be mocked; that which a man soweth, that shall he also reap. And if you will not be at peace with God, God will not be at peace with you. Who can stand before God when he is angry? It is a dreadful thing to fall into the hands of an angry God.

When the people came to apprehend Christ, they fell to the ground when Jesus said, "I am he." And if they could not bear the sight of Christ when clothed with the rags of mortality, how will they hear the sight of him when he is on his Father's throne? Methinks I see the poor wretches dragged out of their graves by the devil; methinks I see them trembling, crying out to the hills and rocks to cover them. But the devil will say come, I will take you away; and then they shall stand trembling before the judgment-seat of Christ. They shall appear before him to see him once and hear him pronounce that irrevocable sentence, "Depart from me, ye cursed." Methinks I hear the poor creatures saying, Lord, if we must be damned, let some angel pronounce the sentence. No, the God of love, Jesus Christ, will pronounce it. Will ye not believe this?

Do not think I am talking at random, but agreeably to the Scriptures of truth. If you do not, then show yourselves men, and this morning go away with full resolution, in the strength of God, to cleave to Christ. And may you have no rest in your souls till you rest in Jesus Christ! I could still go on, for it is sweet to talk of Christ. Do you not long for the time when you shall have new bodies—when they shall be immortal, and made like Christ's glorious body? And then they will talk of Jesus Christ for evermore. But it is time, perhaps, for you to go and prepare for your respective worship, and I would not hinder any of you. My design is to bring poor sinners to Jesus Christ. O that God may bring some of you to himself! May the Lord Jesus now dismiss you with his blessing, and may the dear Redeemer convince you that are unawakened and turn the wicked from the evil of their way! And may the love of God, that passeth all understanding, fill your hearts. Grant this, O Father, for Christ's sake; to whom, with thee and the blessed Spirit, be all honor and glory, now and for evermore. Amen.

APPENDIX 1: SERMONS BY GEORGE WHITEFIELD AND JOHN WESLEY

Sermon by John Wesley—*The Way to the Kingdom*
"The kingdom of God is at hand: repent ye,
and believe the gospel." Mark 1:15

These words naturally lead us to consider, first, the nature of true religion, here termed by our Lord, "the kingdom of God," which, saith he, "is at hand"; and, secondly, the way thereto, which he points out in those words, "Repent ye, and believe the gospel."

I 1. We are, first, to consider the nature of true religion, here termed by our Lord, "the kingdom of God." The same expression the great Apostle uses in his Epistle to the Romans, where he likewise explains his Lord's words, saying, "The kingdom of God is not meat and drink; but righteousness, and peace, and joy in the Holy Ghost" (Rom 14:17).

2. "The kingdom of God," or true religion, "is not meat and drink." It is well known that not only the unconverted Jews, but great numbers of those who had received the faith of Christ, were, notwithstanding "zealous of the law" (Acts 21:20), even the ceremonial law of Moses. Whatsoever, therefore, they found written therein, either concerning meat and drink offerings, or the distinction between clean and unclean meats, they not only observed themselves, but vehemently pressed the same even on those "among the Gentiles who were turned to God"; yea, to such a degree, that some of them taught, wheresoever they came among them, "Except ye be circumcised, and keep the law" (the whole ritual law), "ye cannot be saved" (Acts 15:1, 24).

3. In opposition to these, the Apostle declares, both here and in many other places, that true religion does not consist in meat and drink, or in any ritual observances; nor, indeed in any outward thing whatever; in anything exterior to the heart; the whole substance thereof lying in "righteousness, peace, and joy in the Holy Ghost."

4. Not in any outward thing, such as forms, or ceremonies, even of the most excellent kind. Supposing these to be ever so decent and significant, ever so expressive of inward things; supposing them ever so helpful, not only to the vulgar, whose thought reaches little farther than their sight; but even to men of understanding, men of strong capacities, as doubtless they may sometimes be. Yea, supposing them, as in the case of the Jews, to be appointed by God himself; yet even during the period of time wherein that appointment remains in force, true religion does not principally consist therein; nay, strictly speaking, not at all. How much more must this hold

concerning such rites and forms as are only of human appointment! The religion of Christ rises infinitely higher, and lies immensely deeper, than all these. These are good in their place, just so far as they are in fact subservient to true religion. And it was superstition to object against them, while they are applied only as occasional helps to human weakness. But let no man carry them farther. Let no man dream that they have any intrinsic worth, or that religion cannot subsist without them. This were to make them an abomination to the Lord.

5. The nature of religion is so far from consisting in these; in forms of worship, or rites and ceremonies, that it does not properly consist in any outward actions, of what kind so ever. It is true, a man cannot have any religion who is guilty of vicious, immoral actions; or who does to others what he would not they should do to him, if he were in the same circumstance. And it is also true that he can have no real religion who "knows to do good, and doth it not." Yet may a man both abstain from outward evil, and do good, and still have no religion. Yea, two persons may do the same outward work; suppose, feeding the hungry, or clothing the naked; and, in the meantime, one of these may be truly religious, and the other have no religion at all. For the one may act from the love of God, and the other from the love of praise. So manifest it is, that although true religion naturally leads to every good word and work, yet the real nature thereof lies deeper still, even in "the hidden man of the heart."

6. I say of the heart, for neither does religion consist in orthodoxy, or right opinions; which, although they are not properly outward things, are not in the heart, but the understanding. A man may be orthodox in every point; he may not only espouse right opinions, but zealously defend them against all opposers; he may think justly concerning the incarnation of our Lord, concerning the ever-blessed Trinity, and every other doctrine contained in the oracles of God; he may assent to all the three creeds—that called the Apostles', the Nicene, and the Athanasian; and yet it is possible he may have no religion at all. He may be almost as orthodox as the devil (though, indeed, not altogether; for every man errs in something; whereas we can't well conceive him to hold any erroneous opinion), and may, all the while be as great a stranger as he to the religion of the heart.

7. This alone is religion, truly so called; this alone is in the sight of God of great price. The Apostle sums it all up in three particulars, "righteousness, and peace, and joy in the Holy Ghost." And first, righteousness. We cannot be at a loss concerning this, if we remember the words of our Lord,

describing the two grand branches thereof, on which "hang all the law and the prophets." "Thou shalt love the Lord thy God with all thy heart, and with all thy mind, and with all thy soul, and with all thy strength. This is the first and great commandment" (Mark 12:30); the first and great branch of Christian righteousness. Thou shalt delight thyself in the Lord thy God; thou shalt seek and find all happiness in him. He shall be "thy shield, and thy exceeding great reward," in time and in eternity. All thy bones shall say, "Whom have I in heaven but thee? And there is none upon earth that I desire beside thee!" Thou shalt hear and fulfil His word who saith, "My son, give me thy heart." And, having given him thy heart, thy inmost soul, to reign there without a rival, thou mayest well cry out, in the fullness of thy heart, "I will love thee, O Lord, my strength. The Lord is my strong rock, and my defense; my Savior, my God, and my might, in whom I will trust; my buckler, the horn also of my salvation, and my refuge."

8. And the second commandment is like unto this; the second great branch of Christian righteousness is closely and inseparably connected therewith; even, "Thou shalt love thy neighbor as thyself." Thou shalt love—thou shalt embrace with the most tender good-will, the most earnest and cordial affection, the most inflamed desires of preventing or removing all evil, and of procuring for him every possible good—Thy neighbor—that is, not only thy friend, thy kinsman, or thy acquaintance; not only the virtuous, the friendly, him that loves thee, that prevents or returns thy kindness; but every child of man, every human creature, every soul which God hath made; not excepting him whom thou never hast seen in the flesh, whom thou knowest not, either by face or name; not excepting him whom thou knowest to be evil and unthankful, him that still despitefully uses and persecutes thee; him thou shalt love as thyself; with the same invariable thirst after his happiness in every kind; the same unwearied care to screen him from whatever might grieve or hurt either his soul or body.

9. Now is not this love "the fulfilling of the law"; the sum of all Christian righteousness? Of all inward righteousness, for it necessarily implies "bowels of mercies, humbleness of mind," seeing "love is not puffed up." "Gentleness, meekness, long-suffering," for love "is not provoked," but "believeth, hopeth, endureth all things." And of all outward righteousness, for "love worketh no evil to his neighbor," either by word or deed. It cannot willingly hurt or grieve anyone, and it is zealous of good works. Every lover of mankind, as he hath opportunity, "doth good unto all men," being without partiality and without hypocrisy "full of mercy and good fruits."

10. But true religion, or a heart right toward God and man, implies happiness as well as holiness. For it is not only "righteousness," but also "peace and joy in the Holy Ghost." What peace? "The peace of God," which God only can give, and the world cannot take away; the peace which "passeth all understanding," all barely rational conception; being a supernatural sensation, a divine taste, of "the powers of the world to come"; such as the natural man knoweth not, how wise soever in the things of this world; nor, indeed, can he know it, in his present state, "because it is spiritually discerned." It is a peace that banishes all doubt, all painful uncertainty; the Spirit of God bearing witness with the spirit of a Christian, that he is "a child of God." And it banishes fear, all such fear as hath torment; the fear of the wrath of God; the fear of hell; the fear of the devil; and, in particular, the fear of death; he that hath the peace of God, desiring, if it were the will of God, "to depart, and to be with Christ."

11. With this peace of God, wherever it is fixed in the soul, there is also "joy in the Holy Ghost"; joy wrought in the heart by the Holy Ghost, by the ever-blessed Spirit of God. He it is that worketh in us that calm, humble rejoicing in God, through Christ Jesus, "by whom we have now received the atonement," the reconciliation with God; and that enables us boldly to confirm the truth of the royal Psalmist's declaration, "Blessed is the man" (or rather, happy) "whose unrighteousness is forgiven, and whose sin is covered." He it is that inspires the Christian soul with that even, solid joy, which arises from the testimony of the Spirit that he is a child of God; and that gives him to "rejoice with joy unspeakable, in hope of the glory of God"; hope both of the glorious image of God, which is in part and shall be fully "revealed in him," and of that crown of glory which fadeth not away, reserved in heaven for him.

12. This holiness and happiness, joined in one, are sometimes styled in the inspired writings "the kingdom of God" (as by our Lord in the text), and sometimes "the kingdom of heaven." It is termed "the kingdom of God" because it is the immediate fruit of God's reigning in the soul. So soon as ever he takes unto himself his mighty power, and sets up his throne in our hearts, they are instantly filled with this "righteousness, and peace, and joy in the Holy Ghost." It is called "the kingdom of heaven" because it is (in a degree) heaven opened in the soul. For whosoever they are that experience this, they can aver before angels and men,

> Everlasting life is won,
>
> Glory is on earth begun,

... according to the constant tenor of Scripture, which everywhere bears record, God "hath given unto us eternal life, and this life is in his Son. He that hath the Son" (reigning in his heart) "hath life," even life everlasting (1 John 5:11–12). For "this is life eternal, to know thee, the only true God, and Jesus Christ, whom thou hast sent" (John 17:3). And they, to whom this is given, may confidently address God, though they were in the midst of a fiery furnace,

> Thee, Lord, safe shielded by thy power,
>
> Thee, Son of God, Jehovah, we adore;
>
> In form of man descending to appear:
>
> To thee be ceaseless hallelujahs given,
>
> Praise, as in heaven thy throne, we offer here;
>
> For where thy presence is display'd, is heaven.

13. And this "kingdom of God," or of heaven, "is at hand." As these words were originally spoken, they implied that "the time" was then fulfilled, God being "made manifest in the flesh," when he would set up his kingdom among men, and reign in the hearts of his people. And is not the time now fulfilled? For "Lo! (saith he), I am with you always," you who preach remission of sins in my name, "even unto the end of the world" (Matt 28:20). Wheresoever, therefore, the gospel of Christ is preached, this his "kingdom is nigh at hand." It is not far from every one of you. Ye may this hour enter thereinto, if so be ye hearken to his voice, "Repent ye, and believe the gospel."

II. 1. "This is the way: walk ye in it." And first, "repent"; that is, know yourselves. This is the first repentance, previous to faith; even conviction, or self-knowledge. Awake, then, thou that sleepest. Know thyself to be a sinner, and what manner of sinner thou art. Know that corruption of thy inmost nature, whereby thou art very far gone from original righteousness, whereby "the flesh lusteth" always "contrary to the Spirit," through that "carnal mind" which "is enmity against God," which "is not subject to the law of God, neither indeed can be." Know that thou art corrupted in every power, in every faculty of thy soul; that thou art totally corrupted in every one of these, all the foundations being out of course. The eyes of thine understanding are darkened, so that they cannot discern God, or the things of God. The clouds of ignorance and error rest upon thee and cover thee with the shadow of death. Thou knowest nothing yet as thou oughtest to know, neither God, nor the world, nor thyself. Thy will is no longer the will of God, but is utterly perverse and distorted, averse from all good, from all which God loves, and prone to all evil, to every abomination which God hateth. Thy affections are alienated from God and scattered abroad over all the earth. All thy passions, both thy desires and aversions, thy joys and sorrows, thy hopes and fears, are out of frame, are either undue in their degree, or placed on undue objects. So that there is no soundness in thy soul; but "from the crown of the head, to the sole of the foot" (to use the strong expression of the Prophet), there are only "wounds, and bruises, and putrefying sores."

2. Such is the inbred corruption of thy heart, of thy very inmost nature. And what manner of branches canst thou expect to grow from such an evil root? Hence springs unbelief, ever departing from the living God, saying, "Who is the Lord, that I should serve him? Tush! Thou, God, carest not for it." Hence independence, affecting to be like the Most High. Hence pride, in all its forms, teaching thee to say, "I am rich, and increased in goods, and have need of nothing." From this evil fountain flow forth the bitter streams of vanity, thirst of praise, ambition, covetousness, the lust of the flesh, the lust of the eye, and the pride of life. From this arise anger, hatred, malice, revenge, envy, jealousy, evil surmising. From this, all the foolish and hurtful lusts that now "pierce thee through with many sorrows," and if not timely prevented, will at length drown thy soul in everlasting perdition.

3. And what fruits can grow on such branches as these? Only such as are bitter and evil continually. Of pride cometh contention, vain boasting, seeking and receiving praise of men, and so robbing God of that glory which he cannot give unto another. Of the lust of the flesh, come gluttony or drunkenness, luxury or sensuality, fornication, uncleanness; variously defiling that body which was designed for a temple of the Holy Ghost. Of unbelief, every evil word and work. But the time would fail, shouldst thou reckon up all, all the idle words thou hast spoken, provoking the Most High, grieving the Holy One of Israel; all the evil works thou hast done, either wholly evil in themselves, or, at least, not done to the glory of God. For thy actual sins are more than thou art able to express, more than the hairs of thy head. Who can number the sands of the sea, or the drops of rain, or thy iniquities?

4. And knowest thou not that "the wages of sin is death?"—death, not only temporal, but eternal. "The soul that sinneth, it shall die"; "for the mouth of the Lord hath spoken it." It shall die the second death. This is

the sentence, to "be punished" with never-ending death; "with everlasting destruction from the presence of the Lord, and from the glory of his power." Knowest thou not that every sinner, not properly, "is in danger of hell-fire" is far too weak; but rather, "is under the sentence of hell-fire"; doomed already, just dragging to execution. Thou art guilty of everlasting death. It is the just reward of thy inward and outward wickedness. It is just that the sentence should now take place.

Dost thou see, dost thou feel this? Art thou thoroughly convinced that thou deservest God's wrath, and everlasting damnation? Would God do thee no wrong, if he now commanded the earth to open, and swallow thee up? If thou wert now to go down quick into the pit, into the fire that never shall be quenched? If God hath given thee truly to repent, thou hast a deep sense that these things are so; and that it is of his mere mercy thou art not consumed, swept away from the face of the earth.

5. And what wilt thou do to appease the wrath of God, to atone for all thy sins, and to escape the punishment thou hast so justly deserved? Alas, thou canst do nothing; nothing that will in anywise make amends to God for one evil work, or word, or thought. If thou couldst now do all things well, if from this very hour, till thy soul should return to God thou couldst perform perfect, uninterrupted obedience, even this would not atone for what is past. Thee not increasing thy debt would not discharge it. It would still remain as great as ever. Yea, the present and future obedience of all the men upon earth, and all the angels in heaven, would never make satisfaction to the justice of God for one single sin. How vain, then, was the thought of atoning for thy own sins by anything thou couldest do! It costeth far more to redeem one soul, than all mankind is able to pay. So that were there no other help for a guilty sinner, without doubt he must have perished everlastingly.

6. But suppose perfect obedience, for the time to come, could atone for the sins that are past, this would profit thee nothing, for thou art not able to perform it; no, not in any one point. Begin now, make the trial. Shake off that outward sin that so easily besetteth thee. Thou canst not. How then wilt thou change thy life from all evil to all good? Indeed, it is impossible to be done, unless first thy heart be changed. For, so long as the tree remains evil, it cannot bring forth good fruit. But art thou able to change thy own heart, from all sin to all holiness? To quicken a soul that is dead in sin—dead to God and alive only to the world? No more than thou art able to quicken a dead body, to raise to life him that lieth in the grave. Yea, thou art not able to quicken thy soul in any degree, no more than to give any degree of life

to the dead body. Thou canst do nothing, more or less, in this matter; thou art utterly without strength. To be deeply sensible of this, how helpless thou art, as well as how guilty and how sinful—this is that "repentance not to be repented of," which is the forerunner of the kingdom of God.

7. If to this lively conviction of thy inward and outward sins, of thy utter guiltiness and helplessness, there be added suitable affections—sorrow of heart, for having despised thy own mercies—remorse, and self-condemnation, having thy mouth stopped—shame to lift up thine eyes to heaven—fear of the wrath of God abiding on thee, of his curse hanging over thy head, and of the fiery indignation ready to devour those who forget God, and obey not our Lord Jesus Christ—earnest desire to escape from that indignation, to cease from evil, and learn to do well—then I say unto thee, in the name of the Lord, "Thou art not far from the kingdom of God." One step more and thou shalt enter in. Thou dost "repent." Now, "believe the gospel."

8. The gospel (that is, good tidings, good news for guilty, helpless sinners), in the largest sense of the word means the whole revelation made to men by Jesus Christ; and sometimes the whole account of what our Lord did and suffered while he tabernacled among men. The substance of all is, "Jesus Christ came into the world to save sinners"; or, "God so loved the world that he gave his only-begotten Son, to the end we might not perish, but have everlasting life"; or, "He was bruised for our transgressions, he was wounded for our iniquities; the chastisement of our peace was upon him; and with his stripes we are healed."

9. Believe this, and the kingdom of God is thine. By faith thou attainest the promise. "He pardoneth and absolveth all that truly repent, and unfeignedly believe his holy gospel." As soon as ever God hath spoken to thy heart, "Be of good cheer, thy sins are forgiven thee," his kingdom comes; Thou hast "righteousness, and peace, and joy in the Holy Ghost."

10. Only beware thou do not deceive thy own soul with regard to the nature of this faith. It is not, as some have fondly conceived, a bare assent to the truth of the Bible, of the articles of our creed, or of all that is contained in the Old and New Testament. The devils believe this, as well as I or thou! And yet they are devils still. But it is, over and above this, a sure trust in the mercy of God, through Christ Jesus. It is a confidence in a pardoning God. It is a divine evidence or conviction that "God was in Christ, reconciling the world to himself, not imputing to them their" former "trespasses"; and, in

particular, that the Son of God hath loved me, and given himself for me; and that I, even I, am now reconciled to God by the blood of the cross.

11. Dost thou thus believe? Then the peace of God is in thy heart, and sorrow and sighing flee away. Thou art no longer in doubt of the love of God; it is clear as the noon-day sun. Thou criest out, "My song shall be always of the loving-kindness of the Lord. With my mouth will I ever be telling of thy truth, from one generation to another." Thou art no longer afraid of hell, or death, or him that had once the power of death, the devil; no, nor painfully afraid of God himself; only thou hast a tender, filial fear of offending him. Dost thou believe? Then thy "soul doth magnify the Lord," and thy "spirit rejoiceth in God thy Savior." Thou rejoicest in that thou hast "redemption through his blood, even the forgiveness of sins." Thou rejoicest in that "Spirit of adoption," which crieth in thy heart, "Abba, Father!" Thou rejoicest in a "hope full of immortality"; in reaching forth unto the "mark of the prize of thy high calling," in an earnest expectation of all the good things which God hath prepared for them that love him.

12. Dost thou now believe? Then "the love of God is" now "shed abroad in thy heart." Thou lovest him, because he first loved us. And because thou lovest God, thou lovest thy brother also. And being filled with "love, peace, joy," thou art also filled with "long-suffering, gentleness, fidelity, goodness, meekness, temperance," and all the other fruits of the same Spirit; in a word, with whatever dispositions are holy, are heavenly or divine. For while thou "beholdest with open," uncovered "face" (the veil now being taken away) "the glory of the Lord," his glorious love, and the glorious image wherein thou wast created, thou art "changed into the same image, from glory to glory, by the Spirit of the Lord."

13. This repentance, this faith, this peace, joy, love, this change from glory to glory, is what the wisdom of the world has voted to be madness, mere enthusiasm, utter distraction. But thou, O man of God, regard them not; be thou moved by none of these things. Thou knowest in whom thou hast believed. See that no man take thy crown. Whereunto thou hast already attained, hold fast, and follow, till thou attain all the great and precious promises. And thou who hast not yet known him, let not vain men make thee ashamed of the gospel of Christ. Be thou in nothing terrified by those who speak evil of the things which they know not. God will soon turn thy heaviness into joy. O let not thy hands hang down! Yet a little longer, and he will take away thy fears, and give thee the spirit of a sound mind. He is nigh "that justifieth; Who is he that condemneth? It is Christ that died,

yea rather, that rose again, who is even now at the right hand of God, making intercession" for thee.

"Now cast thyself on the Lamb of God, with all thy sins, how many soever they be"; and "an entrance shall" now "be ministered unto thee, into the kingdom of our Lord and Savior Jesus Christ!"

APPENDIX 2

Additional Great Awakening Sermons[1]

Sermon by Samuel Blair—*The Gospel Method of Salvation; or, The Condemned State of Man by Sin, and the Way Appointed of God for his Recovery Through the Righteousness of Jesus Christ.*

Romans 10:4, "For Christ is the end of the law for righteousness to everyone that believeth."

THESE WORDS SHOW WHAT is the righteousness which God has appointed for the justification of a condemned sinner and for freeing him from the claims and charges of the law against him. We are taught that justification is only to be found in Jesus Christ and consists in what he has done and suffered in the discharge of his mediatorial undertaking, when he was bodily present in this world. The inspired Apostle not only generally declares what the sinners only justifying righteousness is, but particularly characterizes the persons that are actually justified thereby. He points out the great qualification which is prerequisite to justification in telling us that Christ is the end of the law for righteousness to everyone that believes. By these last words he not only extends the benefit of justification to all believers but also limits and restrains it to them only. The point of truth now to be insisted upon is that faith in Christ is necessary in order to [receive] justification by him.

The truth of this proposition is sufficiently attested by the word of God, "He that believeth . . . shall be saved, but he that believeth not shall be damned" (Mark 16:16). "He that believeth on him [the Son] is not condemned, but he that believeth not is condemned already, because he hath

---

1. The sermons within this appendix by Samuel Blair and William Tennent, although edited slightly for this present work, were copied with kind permission from: Roberts, *Salvation in Full Color: Twenty Sermons by Great Awakening Preachers*, 217–231, 289–304.

not believed in the name of the only begotten Son of God" (John 3:18). "He that believeth on the Son hath everlasting life; and he that believeth not the Son shall not see life, but the wrath of God abideth on him" (John 3:36). "We through the Spirit wait for the hope of righteousness by faith. For in Jesus Christ neither circumcision availeth anything, nor uncircumcision; but faith which worketh by love" (Gal 5:5–6). Hence the righteousness of Christ is called the righteousness of faith (Rom 4:11; 10:6) and the righteousness which is of faith (Phil 3:9; Rom 3:22) because of the necessity of faith in order to the soul's saving interest in it.

The method by which I propose to speak of this great truth is: First, to open up a little the nature of faith in Christ and show you what it is. Second, to show you its necessity in the case of a sinner's justification by considering the interest and concern that it has in it. Third, to consider something of the excellency and beauty of this method of a condemned sinner's recovery through faith in the righteousness of Jesus Christ.

I. The nature of true faith in Christ.

True faith is well described in the Shorter Catechism of the Westminster Confession as "a saving grace, whereby we receive and rest upon Christ alone for salvation, as he is freely offered to us in the gospel." Agreeable to this, (that I may speak about it as clearly as I can) take this description of it, "Faith in Christ is a saving grace, whereby a person receives him for his only Saviour, leans and depends upon his righteousness, and that only, for his justification before God, and all things that he stands in need of."

In this description you may especially take notice of these three things: First, a very principal benefit which a person in believing rests upon Christ for is his justification which results in his deliverance from the guilt of sin and condemnation of the law and, consequently, from deserved damnation; and entitles him to eternal happiness and the glory of heaven. This a person in believing, especially in his first closure with Christ, principally respects and has his eyes primarily upon. About this he is most intimately and awfully concerned. But yet he does not stop here. All things that he wants, and all that God has promised, he looks for through Christ alone and that upon account of his mediation; for Christ is the mediator through whom all blessings come from God to his people. Because of this, he directs his disciples to ask whatever they want in his name (John 14:12, 14; 15:16; 16:23, 26). All things that the soul needs are treasured up in Christ the mediator through whom they are communicated to his people. "It pleased the Father that in him should all fullness dwell" (Col 1:19). He is made all things to his people, wisdom, even righteousness, sanctification, and redemption (1 Cor 1:30).

Second, in this description you may observe that, in believing, a person puts trust and confidence in nothing else but Christ for his justification. Thus the holy Apostle disclaims all other trusts, "Yea doubtless, and I count all things but loss for the excellency of the knowledge of Christ Jesus my Lord; for whom I have suffered the loss of all things, and do count them but dung, that I may win Christ, and be found in him, not having my own righteousness, which is of the law, but that which is through the faith of Christ, the righteousness which is of God by faith" (Phil 3:8–9).

Third the soul, in believing, not only rejects all confidences besides Christ but positively and really depends upon the righteousness of Christ for its reconciliation and peace with God. The true believer, as he rejects all other dependence, positively, with a sweet satisfaction of soul, rests on Jesus only. By a positive real act of his soul, he lays hold on him as the only sure foundation and pillar for his sinking soul to be supported and upheld. For this reason, the church is represented as leaning upon her beloved (Song 8:5).

That I may more fully open up to you the nature of faith in Christ as it is revealed in the holy Scriptures, I shall briefly show you:

1. How it is that a believer receives Christ and leans upon his righteousness.
2. That this is the scriptural doctrine concerning justifying faith.
3. The grounds and encouragements upon which the believer, with such satisfaction, leans on Christ and adventures his soul upon him.
4. The higher degree of faith that more effectually frees the soul from anxious fear and mistrust, which a believer may advance to.

1. As to the first, you must consider the terms here generally made use of to signify the soul's exercise of faith in Christ. These terms are not to be understood in a corporal sense, as when we conceive of the leaning of one body upon another. We cannot, in this gross notion, lean or rest on Christ, but the believer relies upon Christ by the assent of his mind and the free conduct of his will. In these two acts of the soul are comprised the whole of saving faith.

a) His assent is nothing else but his firm belief and certain undoubted persuasion of the truth of those things which God has revealed in the Gospels; especially concerning his undone conditions by sin and absolute need of a saviour and concerning the way of recovery and salvation through the righteousness of Christ only. These great truths he certainly and firmly believes, with particular application to himself, so as to be answerably affected by them. He believes them so as to feel the power of them upon his heart, producing those affections and dispositions which they have a native tendency to excite and which the true belief of them will certainly effect. In this assent is necessarily included a distinct knowledge of the things believed.

There can be no true faith in Christ without a competent knowledge of the substance of the gospel. The person that believes in Christ perceives and understands that the report of the gospel is true. He must firmly believe it to be God's truth that by the law of God which he has broken he is a guilty and condemned creature, that he is helpless and undone in himself, and that his only way of relief is through the righteousness of Jesus Christ. To this righteousness he must come and gain an interest in it or perish. He apprehends that Christ has laid no bar against him in the gospel, any more than others, but offers himself a Saviour to the most guilty, wretched, and undone sinners.

b) The second and completing act of faith is the consent of the will. Hereby the poor and humbled sinner freely consents and cheerfully complies to take Christ for his Saviour. He leans the whole weight of his guilty soul and all his eternal concerns upon him. This person, seeing his condemned undone estate by sin, is deeply humbled, made poor in spirit, and altogether stripped and left quite empty in all hopes of relief from himself. Seeing the way of salvation through Christ which is revealed in the gospel, he heartily closes with it and, by a sensible lively act of his soul, receives Christ and leans upon him as his only Saviour. With a sweet satisfaction, he rolls himself upon Christ to save him through the virtue of his merits and continual intercession. He is well pleased with this way of salvation through Christ and lays all his hopes upon him. This faith in Christ is not a mere transient passing act but a settled habit and abiding principle in the soul. It is often, more or less, a sensible feeling exercised in a believer's heart, so that the whole life which he now lives in the flesh he lives by the faith of the Son of God, who loved him and gave himself for him (Gal 2:20).

This knowledge of truth of God's word which discovers the miserable undone condition of the soul without Christ and the way of salvation through his mediation and righteousness, with the powerful belief of it and the hearty unfeigned consent of the will to this way of salvation, whereby the soul freely quits all other holds and sweetly rolls itself over on Jesus Christ, is the sum and substance of saving faith. By these actions of the soul, the believer truly rests and leans on the Son of God, and him only, for his eternal salvation. His eyes are fixed only upon Christ's mediation. The believer makes him the ground of all his hope and the foundation of his confidence towards God.

From these things you may see the reason why this grace is so frequently in Scripture expressed by the terms of knowing, believing and, ordinarily, by this name of faith which properly signifies the believing of some doctrinal proposition and not only by the terms of leaning, depending, trusting, etc. The reason is because it consists in a knowing and believing the gospel revelation of the way of salvation through Christ's righteousness, together with the soul's free and affectionate compliance with it. In this faith, the soul necessarily receives Christ for his Saviour and rests upon him.

Hence also you may see that such as are not firmly persuaded concerning the great foundation truths of the gospel (particularly these which I have shown you) and, even more, such as positively deny and misbelieve them have no true faith in Christ. It is by the believing of these truths that the soul comes to close with the Lord Jesus and to put saving trust in him. There are many who do not dispute these truths and who even give a kind of dead and ineffectual credit to them. They are inclined to believe they are true, but yet for all they know, they may be otherwise. They are far from venturing to lay down their lives upon the truth of them.

It is evident that the faith of such persons is nothing else but doubtful opinion, whereas the language of true faith is that of the disciple, "We believe, and are sure" (John 6:69). This is witnessed by all the holy martyrs of Jesus who have laid down their lives for the truth of the gospel, who were "slain for the word of God, and for the testimony which they held" (Rev 6:9). O Sirs! Here is the great danger and mischief of ignorance in the understanding and of unfixedness and error in the judgment; they keep the soul from union with Christ and dishonor God, for "he that believeth not God hath made him a liar; because he believeth not the record that God gave of his Son. And this is the record, that God hath given us eternal life, and this life is in his Son" (1John 5:10 –11).

2. Having thus far opened the nature of saving faith, I am next to show you that this is the true notion of it taught in the holy Scriptures and that this is the faith which God requires in his word.

a) This is evident in that the wretched, condemned condition of sinners and the way of justification and relief through the virtue of Christ's obedience and sufferings alone is the true Scripture doctrine. Now if these are the truths of God's word, then surely, they are to be believed. And it is certain that the person who truly believes them, in so doing, must necessarily acknowledge and be sensible of his most miserable undone state by sin. He must renounce all confidence in his own righteousness, all trust in himself or anything he can do, and put his whole trust in Christ alone. His whole dependence must be upon Christ's righteousness, for any other trust and dependence would be both contrary to the doctrines of the gospel and inconsistent with real belief in them. Thus, the Lord in the Gospels, offering Christ to sinners as their only Saviour, certainly required them to receive him as such. When this is done really, freely, and affectionately, it is the faith which I have described. So, these doctrines taught in God's word sufficiently discover the nature of true faith in Christ.

b) The Scriptures hold forth the nature of faith by such expressions as necessarily and clearly fix it to this believing dependence upon Christ's righteousness, "Being justified freely by his grace through the redemption that is in Christ Jesus, whom God has set forth to be a propitiation through faith in his blood" (Rom 3:24–25). Faith in his blood here plainly signifies a dependence upon his death and sufferings as the only price of our redemption, and peace with God as that through which a condemned sinner must be justified. It can mean nothing else. To this purpose the Apostle Paul declared the nature of his faith, expressing his entire dependence upon the mediatorial righteousness of Christ and renouncing all trust in any other righteousness (Phil 3). After he had particularly related his strict legal righteousness and personal advantages in the former part of the chapter, he says "What things were gain to me, those I counted loss for Christ" (verse 7). It is as if he had said, "Those things I have just related and all others like them, which I at one time highly valued and counted on to gain heaven, are but as dross without Christ. I quit all dependence upon them for him for whom I have suffered the loss of all things, and do count them but dung, that I may win Christ; and be found in him, not having mine own righteousness which is of the law, but that which is through the faith of Christ" (verses 8–9). In a word, Paul reveals the nature of his justifying faith when he says,

"Christ has redeemed us from the curse of the law, (by) being made a curse for us." The Lord Jesus Christ himself shows this to be the nature of faith in him when he speaks of it under the notion of eating his flesh and drinking his blood (John 6:51).

3. I now endeavor to show you how a person comes to put such trust in the Lord Jesus; upon what ground and encouragement he leans on Christ with such satisfaction and peace so as, rejecting all other dependence, to adventure his guilty soul wholly on him.

a) Negatively—You must consider that he takes no encouragement from the consideration of any peculiar privileges or personal righteousness of his own. He does not think thereby to recommend himself to Christ or render himself in any way worthy of his righteousness. That would be just another way of seeking justification by works or by personal righteousness. It would be laying the foundation of faith upon something in ourselves and not entirely upon Christ.

b) Affirmatively—The progress of faith in Christ is much according to these several steps:

1) The soul sees that he is brought into a miserable and condemned state by sin. He finds that he is forever a most undone creature unless he can find some way of relief wherein he can obtain a full removal of his awful guilt and a total discharge of his obligation to a punishing and vindictive justice.

2) He sees and is sure that there is no other way of relief for him but through the mediation and righteousness of the Redeemer Christ, according to the Scriptures (John 14:6; Acts 4:12; Rom 3:20–26).

3) He conceives a strong probability of finding relief this way, a probability of peace with God and of escaping God's wrath through Christ's righteousness. He perceives that God will receive him in his love and mercy; poor, wretched and hell-deserving as he is, in his beloved Son. This encouragement and ground of trust in Christ he takes not from any conceit of worthiness in himself or in his own doings which will recommend his acceptance, but from the all-sufficiency and fullness which he discovers in Christ himself and the free offer of Christ in the gospel. He sees that Christ is truly an all-sufficient Saviour, able to save them to the uttermost that come to God by him. He sees that Christ has offered himself for sin, a sacrifice of infinite value, having poured out his soul unto death. But he also sees that Christ has risen again from the dead, ascended up into glory, sits at the right hand of the majesty on high, and now ever lives to make intercession

for him. He discovers, likewise, that Christ is offered fully and freely in the gospel as a Saviour for the most unworthy and hell-deserving, "Ho, everyone that thirsteth, come ye to the waters; and he that hath no money, come ye, buy and eat, yea, come, buy wine and milk without money and without price" (Isa 55:1); "Come unto me, all ye that labor and are heavy laden, and I will give you rest" (Matt 11:28). Now surely here is encouragement enough for the convinced sinner to receive Christ and a sufficient foundation for his trust in him.

And thus the poor humbled soul, seeing that he is miserable and undone by sin and that there is no other way of relief or help for him and that there is a high probability of hope this way considering the sufficiency of the Redeemer and the freeness of his offers, lets go all other dependence and resolves to venture himself entirely upon the Lord Jesus. To Christ he will cleave, and he will not let him go. Because there is no one else who can help him, he is like a man among the devouring waves in the open ocean who lays hold upon a single plank which he will not part with, utterly despairing of help in any other way.

Sometimes the case of the soul in believing is much like that of the four lepers at the gate of Samaria at the time the city suffered a siege from an enemy without and a cruel famine within. "And there were four leprous men at the entering in of the gate; and they said one to another, 'Why sit we here until we die?' If we say, 'We will enter into the city,' then the famine is in the city, and we shall die there; and if we sit still here, we die also. Now therefore come and let us fall into the host of the Syrians; if they save us alive, we shall live; and if they kill us, we shall but die" (2 Kgs 7:3–4). These men, in their extremity, had some probability of help from the Syrians in their view, but gave up all hope any other way. The truly humbled sinner sees himself in the same strait, but he has much more ground offered him in the gospel to trust in Christ for his relief than these men had to confide in the Syrian army. He considers, like them, that if he sits still where he is, he shall die; if he continues in that condemned state in which he is without Christ, he shall surely die. If he goes anywhere else but to Christ, he shall die there. If he trusts in his own righteousness, depends upon his personal obedience and reformation, that cannot save him, but he shall die there also. Thus, being reduced to the greatest extremity and beholding the glorious encouragement opened in the gospel of relief and help in Jesus Christ, he joyfully lays hold on him as his Saviour, and there he rests his weary soul.

This saving faith is called the faith of adherence or dependence only. It falls short of a bright and full assurance. Yet it has very precious and sweet effects; it causes the soul to dart out the beams of pure and transcendent love to the glorious God; it introduces a sweet joy into the soul; it brings a balmy peace to the wounded conscience in proportion to the degree of faith and trust which the soul reposes in Jesus Christ. I pray you to compare these things with the experiences of your own souls and examine whether you ever have so received Christ.

O Sirs! It is so important to be truly sensible of your utter undoneness without Christ and of your absolute need of him. Nothing else can help the condemned sinner! Without a sense of this lostness, it is impossible to come to Christ. Without this, the soul is not even in the way to believe in him. Although a conviction of a sinner's misery and of the depth of his poverty of spirit renders the sinner no more worthy of Christ, yet it is necessary to put the soul in the way to truly embrace Christ and believe in him.

4. There is yet a higher degree of faith, a more full and sweet recumbency on the Lord Jesus that more effectually frees the soul from anxious fear and mistrust, which a believer may advance to and for which he has answerable ground and encouragement from God. The God of truth, who cannot deceive, has positively promised that whosoever comes to Christ in this manner and leans his guilty soul wholly upon him, be he ever so vile, poor, and unworthy, shall be accepted in him. What a blessed assurance is that which Christ himself, the Lord of life gives, "All that the Father giveth me shall come to me, and him that cometh to me, I will in no wise cast out" (John 6:37). Then in verse forty, he assures us that it is the Father's will and pleasure that all who believe in him shall be eternally saved, "And this is the will of him that sent me, that everyone which seeth the Son, and believeth on him, may have everlasting life; and I will raise him up at the last day." What a sweet word this is to a believer, "Behold, I lay in Zion a chief corner-stone, elect, precious; and he that believeth on him shall not be confounded" (1 Pet 2:6). Now when the poor and humble soul discovers this, he receives Christ and leans upon him with the greater confidence; for he has the sure word of God for his warrant and the infallible promises of Jehovah for the foundation of his faith. When the believer sees his security as consisting in his having been accepted in Christ and in faith lays hold thereupon until he is sensibly filled with the realization of his position in Christ, then it is the faith of assurance. By this faith one is as sure that God is reconciled to him in Christ as that there is a God or that he himself lives upon the earth.

Thus, I have laid before you the nature of a true and saving faith. From what has been said you may conceive how humble, low, and base in his own sight a true believer is; how deeply sensible of his wretchedness and poverty in himself. Hence you may see what a strong and unspeakable love must needs fill his heart towards the gracious God who has provided such a remedy for so undone and vile a creature. His heart burns within him with the purest love to the divine majesty! How exceeding dear is Christ to his soul! Well might the Apostle say, "To you that believe, he is precious" (1 Pet 2:7). Christ is to him as the apple tree among the trees of the wood (Song 2:3). His very name is an ointment poured forth (Song 1:3). What a sweet peace and satisfaction possesses his soul in leaning upon his Saviour! In a word, how freely and fully does he give himself up to Christ, to serve him while he lives, to be for him, and none else, forever.

II. I proceed to show you the necessity of faith in Christ for justification through his righteousness.

That it is indispensably necessary to this end is beyond dispute with all that understand and believe the Scriptures; but I am to consider upon what account it is so necessary, what is the concern which it has in the justification of a sinner, and why he cannot be justified without it. Here, then, you must know that faith is not concerned in justification as a qualification that is in any way meritorious of it. Nothing has any hand or part in justification as a merit or price but the righteousness of the Lord Jesus. His merit is so full and sufficient that nothing else is necessary. To Christ belongs the whole honor and praise for the purchase of salvation.

But faith is concerned in justification as the hand or instrument which receives the righteousness of Christ and applies it to the soul according to the wise constitution and appointment of God in the gospel. Upon this account, it is necessary to justification. By faith the soul lays hold on Christ as its Saviour, and as the believer receives Christ and depends upon his righteousness, the Lord then imputes Christ's righteousness to him. The righteousness of Christ is placed upon the believer's account as fully as if he had produced a righteousness of his own. The Lord now looks upon it as the believer's righteousness, he having laid hold upon it as his only justifying righteousness and having put all his hopes in it. This is the way which the Lord has appointed for the sinner's interest in Christ's justifying righteousness, by his receiving and laying hold upon it by faith. A man may as soon be saved from drowning by a plank in the water which he will not lay hold upon, and a beggar may as soon be enriched by alms offered him while refusing to put forth his hand to receive it, as a person can be justified by Christ without receiving him by faith. And indeed, it cannot in reason be expected that any should be benefitted by the gospel method of grace and salvation without their hearty compliance with it. The Lord will save none in any way against their wills; and none do consent and agree to this way of salvation through Christ which God has appointed until they embrace Christ and close with him by faith. Those that still wish to be saved some other way cannot be saved, for there is no other way. Therefore, if you agree not unfeignedly to this, you are eternally undone.

III. I propose to lay before you something of the glory and excellency of this method which God has established for the justification of a condemned sinner.

Since its beauty consists of two parts, the merits of Christ's atonement and faith in the same on our part, I shall consider it in both these respects.

1. The meritorious cause of justification is the obedience and suffering of the Son of God. The gospel scheme of salvation is in every way worthy of God, for in it his adorable perfections receive a very marvelous display. How glorious does his infinite wisdom appear in it!

The law of God, or the first covenant treaty of God with man, requires a perfect obedience in all things and at all times as the condition of eternal life. The total condition must be fulfilled, or eternal life cannot be obtained. But mankind has come universally short and so is condemned to the terrible misery of the loss of glory and happiness forever. Because of non-performance of the condition of life, man is shut out of heaven and deprived of a glorious immortality by this first covenant. Upon consideration of his transgressing the law of God he is, according to the tenor of this covenant, condemned to that positive punishment which his sin deserves, which is very dreadful and unspeakable, and which must be sustained. Now, man is utterly incapable of answering these demands of the law for his recovery; and there is no other creature able to answer the law for him or willing to undertake it. Which way then shall the law be answered and the sinner relieved? He cannot answer it himself any other way than by suffering eternally.

But supposing he could, in a limited duration, bear all that positive punishment which the law doomed him to for his sin. Yet even then he could have no access to the glorious enjoyment of God because he had failed in his obedience and had not fulfilled the condition upon which this happiness was promised. How then shall both the law be answered and the poor sinner saved? Would not this one question have put the whole creation to silence and eternally non-plussed the highest reach of creature-thoughts?

The resolution of it exceeds the utmost bounds of all creature invention. It would appear utterly impossible that the law could be answered any other way than by the sinner's falling a sacrifice to vindictive justice. But behold and admire the astonishing wisdom of Jehovah, whereby he has made foolish the wisdom of the world. The second person in the glorious Godhead, the eternal Son of God, who is God equal with the Father, takes upon himself our nature and thereby becomes capable of fulfilling the law which sinners had broken and bearing its awful penalty. The infinite dignity of his person adds an infinite value to his mediation so that the law is fully answered in the utmost of its demands and a door of hope is opened for guilty and wretched creatures. Oh, astonishing mystery! "And without controversy great is the mystery of godliness; God was manifest in the flesh" (1 Tim 3:16). Though a crucified Christ be to the Jews a stumbling block and to the Greeks foolishness, yet to them that are called, whether Jews or Greeks, he is the power of God and the wisdom of God (1 Cor 1:23–24). Such wisdom astonishes all the saints on earth as well as all the hosts of heaven. Infinite wisdom shines all around this amazing scheme, such wisdom that it strikes us with astonishment and wonder when we behold it.

What a strange and wonderful method God proposed to answer the law and to save the condemned sinner by the union of God and man in one person, so that "Wonderful" is justly put as the first part of our Emmanuel's name (Isa 9:6). How difficult and even impossible for a created understanding to discovery any method sufficient to accomplish this great end; but it was no difficulty for God. He has found a ransom, and how fit and sufficient is the means proposed for the obtaining of the end designed. The unspotted holiness and inflexible justice of God are clearly manifested in this method of salvation. Herein he has testified concerning the dreadful desert of sin and of his infinite abhorrence of it. Rather than allow it to go unpunished, he punished it in his own dear Son and so maintained the honor and awful respect due to his royal law.

But think also how gloriously the infinite love of God and the riches of his grace and compassion are declared in it! Oh, admirable love, that God should give his own well-beloved Son a sacrifice for hell-deserving sinners; that the Son of God should stoop so low to save rebellious worms! O Sirs! How this thought does endear God to his people and enflame their hearts with a returning love to him! By this method of salvation, God not only eminently displays his sweetest glory to his people but highly endears himself unto their hearts, even above the angels who have only to sing the praises of creating goodness. But his people shall sing the praises of redeeming love to the Father, Son, and Holy Ghost forever, while they behold the Lamb that was slain in the midst of the throne of God.

How dreadfully then do they err who, to the dishonor of God and the ruin of their own souls, from a conceit of raising religion to a very sublime height of spirituality, look upon a crucified Jesus as too mean and carnal a thing to be the object of a believer's faith or to have his heart much influenced and affected by it. This is some spirituality indeed that so undervalues and despises the most glorious expression of the divine perfections that ever the world was acquainted with and the most beautiful scene that was ever opened to the view of God's rational creation. Such is the method of redemption through a crucified Saviour; and such as are truly spiritually enlightened see it so. Though Christ crucified be to others foolishness, to them that believe, he is the power of God and the wisdom of God. "For God, who commanded the light to shine out of darkness, hath shined in our hearts, to give the light of the knowledge of the glory of God in the face of Jesus Christ" (2 Cor 4:6).

2. As to faith, the instrumental cause of justification, the gospel method of salvation appears amiable and beautiful in that faith in Christ is therein made the indispensable necessity for the application of his righteousness to the soul. Is it not very becoming that a guilty and vile creature, deserving of God's wrath, should be sensible to whom he is beholden for his salvation, especially when it has been purchased for him at so dear a rate and, in order that he should give the whole glory and praise to the Author of it, to take to himself shame and confusion of face? Is it not reasonable that the Lord Jesus should have the whole glory of redemption given to him by his redeemed ones? Now these things are only provided for by this appointment of faith. Without faith Christ should not have the just honors of his mediation paid to him. The unbeliever always robs him of them.

Then again, by this constitution of the necessity of faith, there is a provision made for the sanctification and holiness of those who are justified by Christ. Had there been no provision made this way in the gospel method of justification, had provision only been made for the salvation of sinners from the punishment of hell and not also from the power and dominion of sin, this had been a stain and blemish on it, and it would have marred all its beauty. But faith in Christ has a powerful influence upon holiness of life, as clearly appears from its very nature as I have before explained to you. For faith endears Christ to the soul and fills it with pure love to his majesty. It works by love, as the Apostle tells us (Gal 5:6), and love works by obedience. A person that truly loves Christ, delights to honor and please him by obeying his commandments. This Jesus himself tells us, "If a man loves me, he will keep my words" (John 14:23). A total rejecting of all dependence upon our obedience and entire dependence upon Christ is the surest foundation of obedience and the only principle from whence a pure obedience flows. God regards not that mercenary obedience which blind sinners perform from a legal principle, thinking by their faithless, graceless services to recommend themselves to the acceptance of the Holy God. When obedience flows from this spring, it is no true obedience to God. He detests and abhors it! The only obedience that is pleasing in his sight is that which proceeds from a pure love, kindled by the grace of faith.

Application.

Now, my hearers, I entreat you to examine yourselves whether you have true faith in Christ or not. You have heard the absolute necessity of it, that without it you never can be saved. You have heard the nature of it laid open. Now then, I beseech you to search your own souls to ascertain whether you are true believers in Christ. Have you ever been thoroughly convinced of your guilty and condemned state of sin so as to be deeply distressed because of it? Have you rejected all other things and quitted all dependence upon everything else and laid hold on the Lord Jesus for your soul's salvation, depending upon him alone for it, through the virtue of his merits and mediatorial works? Have you received him by such a faith as makes him exceeding dear and precious to your hearts? Is he dearer to you than your own lives so that it is the unfeigned and fervent desire and endeavor of your souls to serve him in all ways and obey him in all his laws?

Such of you as have closed with Jesus Christ have great ground of comfort, for he that believeth on the son hath everlasting life. But you who have not so received Christ are yet in your condemned state. This moment you are under the wrath of God. All your numberless sins stand in force against you unforgiven; not one of them is pardoned. Divine justice is every day ready to take vengeance on your guilty heads. There is nothing that stands between you and its dismal strokes but the mere longsuffering and forbearance of the gracious God. Even this will be worn out in time, and his fiery wrath being once kindled against you, the Lord will pursue you in his fury and precipitate your ever-rebellious and stubborn souls into the deepest hell for ever. And then you shall see (but alas! too late) what a dreadful thing it was that you did not come to Christ. He that believeth not, says Christ, shall be damned.

Farther, you that believe in Jesus Christ, let me entreat you, dear brethren, to be much in the exercise of this precious grace of faith so that you may say with the Apostle, "The life which I now live in the flesh, I live by the faith of the Son of God" (Gal 2:20). This is the way to honor God and to get comfort in your own souls. You should be frequently looking by faith to Jesus, the Captain of your salvation, and leaning your souls upon him. You should endeavor to strengthen your faith by considering that he that believeth on him shall not be confounded. He is an able and all-sufficient Saviour, "able to save them to the utmost that come unto God by him, seeing he ever liveth to make intercession for them" (Heb 7:25).

And you who have never received Christ by faith, I call to you from the great God now to hasten to the Lord Jesus and to throw yourselves at his feet, craving for his mercy. I plead with you to depend wholly and solely on him for your salvation if you do not choose to be eternally undone. There are two things which are the greatest hindrances in the way of sinners coming to Christ—First, an insensibleness of their extreme need of him. Many sinners do not see that wretched condition which they are in without him. They will not be convinced of it; therefore, they sit still at ease and will not come to Christ for relief while they are not aware of their misery. Secondly, when they are in some measure sensible of their undone condition, they are often seeing relief in a wrong method, depending upon their great reformation, their repentance and their obedience for it. There they take sanctuary for themselves, short of Christ.

Now I have endeavored to remove these two undoing evils which keep the souls from Christ. I have shown you that condemned wretched state which sin has brought you into and the only way of recovery out of it, through Jesus Christ. What can I do more? I beseech you to consider these things and lay them solemnly to heart. I call heaven and earth to witness against you this day, that I have shown you the only way in which you may escape eternal perdition, the way in which you may flee from the wrath to come. By getting an interest through faith in the dearest Redeemer, you may be made happy creatures both in time and eternity. Oh, why then would you be resolved to die in your sins? May the Lord, the high and Holy God, follow with his powerful blessing what has been spoken to your true conversion to Christ, that your souls may be saved in the day of the Lord Jesus. Amen.

APPENDIX 2: ADDITIONAL GREAT AWAKENING SERMONS

Sermon by William Tennent—
An Exhortation to Walk in Christ

"As ye have therefore received Christ Jesus the Lord,
so walk ye in him." Col 2:6

The best of men may fall into errors both in doctrine and practice. This is a truth so incontestably evident that it cannot be denied by any who are in the least acquainted either with their own hearts or sacred and human history. Those who know themselves find, to their sorrow, a root of bitterness and unbelief in themselves inclining them to depart from the living God (Heb 3:12). Those who know history find it abounds with pregnant proofs of this sad truth in the awful accounts it provides of the slips and falls of men whose sincerity and integrity is beyond all doubt. For examples we have only to consider Noah, Lot, Abraham, David, or Peter. Thus, we may wisely say with King David, "Verily, every man at his best estate is altogether vanity" (Ps 39:5).

This our Apostle well knew; and although he was fully persuaded that the faith of the brethren at Colossi was not feigned and hypocritical but true and genuine as is clear from verse five, he yet saw it necessary to exhort them to cautious diligence and persevering progress in their Christian course in the words of our text, "As ye have therefore received Christ Jesus the Lord, so walk ye in him."

In this text we have these three things:

1. The means of their steadfastness pointed to.

2. The manner in which they ought to be used.

3. An argument to enforce the exhortation.

Consider each of these in their order.

1. We have the means of steadfastness or perseverance mentioned in the word walk. This expression is metaphorical and has an allusion to a person traveling to a certain place which he will never reach unless he continues to go forward. The word is to be understood as an exhortation to constant progress in religion. The Apostle Peter expresses it as "Grow in grace, and in the knowledge of our Lord and Saviour Jesus Christ" (2 Pet 3:18). Without this continued walk, believers will not be able to withstand the beguiling enticements they will meet which will seek to draw them from their spiritual resolutions (Col 2:4).

2. We have an account of the manner in which this means should be used, "so walk Ye in him."

a) We must walk in the way of his commandments. God's law is the rule according to which the whole life must be squared. "To the law and to the testimony, if they speak not according to this word, it is because there is no light in them" (Isa 8:20). This is that sure word of prophecy to which we must give heed for direction in the course of our practice, as to a light shining in a dark place (2 Pet 1:19). We must not offer to undertake anything that we cannot see is agreeable to and approved by the holy Scriptures.

b) We must walk in his strength. We must not trust to ourselves in any case nor to our own wisdom to direct us in any of our affairs, whether civil or religious, our wisdom being foolishness with God (2 Cor 3:19). We must not trust in our power to support us in doing the duties required of us or as a shield to protect us from the assaults of enemies which we will undoubtedly meet with in the way of obedience, it being but weakness itself, "for without me ye can do nothing" (John 15:5). We must not trust in the sincerity and firmness of our resolutions to carry us on in the Christian course, for "he that trusteth in his own heart is a fool" (Prov 28:26). None of these things just mentioned, although exercised in the best manner, can support the soul under one attack by our great enemy; therefore the wise man advises, "Trust in the Lord with all thine heart; and lean not unto thine own understanding. In all thy ways acknowledge him, and he shall direct thy paths" (Prov 3:5–6). In a word, to walk in Christ is to look wholly to him for wisdom, righteousness, sanctification, and redemption (1 Cor 1:30), giving him the glory for all that we have or are as the holy Apostle says, "By the grace of God, I am what I am." We must do all things with an aim to honor him, "Whether therefore ye eat, or drink, or whatsoever ye do, do all to the glory of God" (1 Cor 10:31).

3. The argument by which this duty is enforced is taken from their having received Christ. "As ye have therefore received Christ Jesus the Lord, so walk ye in him." He does not say that they had received only the doctrine of Christ but his person also, as in John 1:12, "But as many as received him, to them gave he power to become the sons of God. . . ." He does not say that they had taken him only as a Saviour but as a sovereign and Lord, to rule and govern them. Seeing the Colossians had before consented to the terms of the gospel in accepting Christ as a Prophet to instruct them, a Priest to atone for them, and a King to govern them; they were therefore obliged by solemn covenant contract to continue their subjection to his commanding

authority as well as to rest their entire dependence upon his merit and influence. The Apostle not only urges the necessity of their walking in Christ because they had received him but also of doing it after the same manner as if he had said, "With the same seriousness, humility, esteem, and resolution with which ye at first receivd Christ, ye should continue to walk in him, for he is now as precious as ever."

Doctrine: It is the duty of all those that have received the Lord Jesus Christ to walk in him.

The doctrine needs no proof, it being the words of the text. In speaking to which, I shall (God willing) observe the following method, namely: First, I shall enquire how every one that has Christ does receive him? Second, show when persons may be said to walk so as to comply with the design of this text. Third, show the advantages of this way of walking. Fourth, apply the whole in some practical uses.

I. I enquire how everyone that has Christ does receive him.

In general, they receive him as he is offered in the gospel, for none shall have him otherwise. The terms he has already unalterably fixed, for he is a God that changes not (Mal 3:6). You may read the terms yourselves, "He that loveth father or mother more than me is not worthy of me, and he that loveth son or daughter more than me is not worthy of me. And he that taketh not his cross, and followeth after me, is not worthy of me. He that findeth his life shall loose it, and he that loseth his life for my sake shall find it" (Matt 10:37–39). The evangelist Luke proposes the same terms (14:26–27) and peremptorily excludes all that have not complied with them from being disciples of Christ. Read the text, dear brethren! Try yourselves by it, whether or not you have gone so far that the love you bear to father, mother, wife, children, yes, to your own life, is so much short of that love you have for God that when compared with, it appears as hatred? And are you deliberately and habitually resolved to forsake these when called to it, as willingly as a man abandons a thing he hates? Now, if it is not so with you, I assure you, in God's name, that you neither are nor ever can be Christ's disciples if you so continue.

1. Christ is received with understanding.

a) We must understand ourselves and our own undoneness, both by nature and act. The poor prodigal said, "I perish with hunger" (Luke 15:17). We must understand our inability to help ourselves out of our undone condition by all the prayers, tears, or other duties we either have or can perform; but that instead we run more in debt to injured justice, for, when we have done all these things, we must say, "we are unprofitable servants" (Luke 17:10).

b) We must understand the necessity, suitableness, and excellency of Jesus Christ for our relief out of that damnable state into which by sin we brought ourselves. "Neither is there salvation in any other, for there is none other name under heaven given among men, whereby we must be saved" (Acts 4:12). Without this knowledge, both of Christ and ourselves, no man can receive him as a Saviour. And let them speak of him ever so favorably, none have an interest in Christ unless they heard and learned of the Father before coming to Christ (John 6:45).

2. Christ is received with real sincerity and with unfeigned faith (1 Tim 1:5). It is from necessity and not out of compliment that the poor soul receives him. Their case is like that of the manslayer under the law who was at a distance from the city of refuge and under the hourly expectation of a mortal stroke from the hand of the blood-avenger. With eager haste and unwearied travel, he rushes to the sanctuary for shelter, lest he should fall prey to the destroyer's rage. So it is with those who receive Christ. They see justice pursuing them for satisfaction for the wrong done to God. They are really afraid that it will overtake them before they are interested in the Saviour. This makes the soul solemnly serious in the act of reception!

3. Christ is received wholly, in all his offices, as Prophet, Priest, and King. They are convinced that unless he had been so qualified he would not have answered as a Saviour for them, because they labor under a threefold difficulty of ignorance, guilt and weakness, each of which grievously presses them and from which they groan for deliverance. It doesn't satisfy the truly godly just to have sin pardoned. Unless its power is broken, they have no ease. "O wretched man that I am! Who shall deliver me from the body of this death?" (Rom 7:24). Neither will this satisfy unless they are taught how to conduct themselves in the future; therefore does the Psalmist pray, "Teach me thy way, O Lord; I will walk in thy truth" (Ps 86:11).

Hypocrites are not so. If they can get Christ to save them from the bottomless, burning lake which some of them justly fear will be their everlasting dwelling place, they could easily dispense with his prophetical and kingly offices. As for their ignorance, it never much troubled them, they being wise in their own conceit, as are both the fool and the sluggard (Prov 26:16). Or, if their ignorance is detected, they then please themselves with the abuse of Luke 12:48, "For unto whomsoever much is given, of him shall much be required." They hypocritically say, "I have but little, therefore only a little will be required of me." But however unreasonable this way of arguing is, it serves to keep them from Christ as Prophet. Now, lest any of my hearers should continue to bolster themselves up in their ignorance by the abuse of the aforementioned text, I offer a word more upon it; "Unto whomsoever" refers to the measure of understanding that he gives us and the opportunities that are ours to improve this power in obtaining divine knowledge. God requires us to make an increase of the understanding he gives, for though knowledge be a gift of God, yet it is given as means to be utilized, and for this reason, it is ordinarily given. Therefore, those who neglect to improve opportunities offered them are utterly inexcusable. For this is "a people of no understanding; therefore he that made them will not have mercy on them, and he that formed them will show them no favor" (Isa 27:11).

Neither do hypocrites, from their hearts, desire Christ as a King to rule over them entirely. No! Their right eyes and right hands are too dear to them to pluck out and cut off for his sake. In the meantime, there are none more full of lip-devotion than they. They cry, "Hail master, and Lord, Lord!" But it is all a mere sham and court-compliment, for "they will not have him to rule over them," and so, not taking a whole Saviour, they have no Saviour at all.

4. Christ is received as the only Saviour and all points of dependence other than him are rejected. "Neither is there salvation in any other; for there is none other name under heaven given among men, whereby we must be saved" (Acts 4:12).

Believers reject all other points of dependence deliberately, having sufficiently tried the worth and weight of all their privileges and performances (which probably they were wont to value highly) and found them of no more worth to their justification than dung and dross. Then do they desire with holy Paul, to be found in him, not having their "own righteousness which is of the law, but that which is through the faith of Christ, the righteousness which is of God through faith" (Phil 3:9). But it is time I should proceed to show—

II. When persons may be said to walk so as to comply with the design of the Apostle in our text.

1. This they may be said to do when they walk in the way of God's commandments with diligence and activity, making religion their chief business and employment. Christ commanded, "Seek ye first the kingdom of God and his righteousness" (Matt 6:33). The seeking of God's kingdom is to be first in the order of time, in the morning of your life. "Remember now thy Creator in the days of thy youth" (Eccl 12:1). It is to be first in point of dignity, as that which is infinitely more valuable that all other things. It is to be first in respect to diligence; it should be sought after with the greatest application and intention of mind. Thus, the godly are said to meditate in the law of God day and night (Ps 1:2).

All earthly things ought to be sought after with indifference when compared with the pains used in seeking Christ. So, the Apostles advises to "buy as though they possessed not" (1 Cor 7:30); but alas, this is ordinarily practiced the backward way. They pray as if they prayed not, hear as if they had not heard, etc. A spirit of indifference runs through all the veins of their religious performances. Yea, while they are burning hot in pursuit of the world, they are as cold as a stone in the service of God. These hypocrites the Lord complains of in Matthew 15:7–8, which passage I plead with you to read at your leisure. Try yourselves by it that you may not go down to the pit with a lie in your right hand, thinking you serve God when you do but play the hypocrite in complimenting him with good words while your hearts ordinarily run after your covetousness and that without trouble or grief for it. If this be the case of any of you, as I fear it is of many in this assembly, the Lord tells you as particularly as if he had mentioned you by name in that text already cited that you are but rotten-hearted hypocrites and therefore not of those that walk according to the exhortation in our text.

2. This they may be said to do when they go on in the duties of piety with freedom and cheerfulness. "I delight to do thy will, O my God; yea, thy law is within my heart" (Ps 40:8). Believers take great delight in the ways of God, esteeming them infinitely more desirable than the best of all created comforts, as did holy David, "More to be desired are they than gold, yea, than much fine gold; sweeter also than honey and the honeycomb" (Ps 19:10). As real holiness is more valuable to the enlightened mind than the finest gold, so it is sweeter to the renewed taste than honey from the comb. The Psalmist seemed to be in almost an ecstatic rapture when he said, "I was glad when they said unto me, let us go into the house of the Lord" (Ps

122:1), and he expressed his satisfaction in and advantage by it in Ps 73:28 in saying, "It is good for me to draw near to God."

But on the other hand, such as are ordinarily drawn to secret, private, or public worship involuntarily rather count it a burden than a delight. Such is the language of those whose souls are described in Amos 8:5, "When will the new moon be gone, that we may sell corn, and the Sabbath, that we may set forth wheat?" All those who count the service of God a weariness and excuse themselves in the neglect of the duties of religion may thereby know themselves to be slaves and not sons, else their obedience would not be of constraint but free.

3. Persons may be said to comply with the exhortation when they act in religion deliberately; that is, when their religious progress is the effect of due consideration and choice. "I have chosen the way of truth: thy judgments have I laid before me" (Ps 119:30). Here it is as if the Psalmist said, "I have thoroughly weighed the advantages that would accompany a right following of thy ways with the disadvantages and found that cleaving to God is beneficial and reasonable; therefore, I will not soon retreat from my duty." "I have stuck unto thy testimonies, O Lord" (119:31). The want of this sticking is the reason why so many apostatize from their profession. Many inconsiderately take up their profession, not counting what it will or might cost them, and they as quickly lay it down rather than suffer for it. As our Lord says, "afterward, when affliction or persecution ariseth for the word's sake, immediately they are offended" (Mark 4:17).

That there are multitudes of these inconsiderate souls under the gospel, who take up their religion only by custom, education, or some good mood, is clearly evident, not only by the many sad instances of persons apostatizing from the precious doctrines and pious practices which they formerly adhered to but also by the inability of many (who have not yet made such woeful shipwreck) to render a reason for the hope that is in them, with meekness and fear, although it is a duty commanded (1 Pet 3:15).

4. Such as walk in Christ are constant in their religious performances, the general tenor of their lives being spent this way. There are some who serve God by fits and starts. At a sacramental season you can hardly find anybody more zealous and fervent in duty, or on the Sabbath; but as soon as the task is done (for so they esteem attendance upon God in his ordinances), they are at ease and so lay down their watch and return to their old trade of sinning again. Fear of punishment drives them to worship but does not change their hearts; therefore they return to their old Delilahs

until the next public occasion; and so they go on in a continued vicissitude of duty and sin, not considering that if they regard iniquity in their hearts, the Lord will not hear their prayers although God Himself has told them so (Ps 66:18). Are there any in this congregation who act in the aforesaid manner? If there be, I assure them, be they who they will, that they rather walk in Satan than in Christ. Hence, the Apostle directs his brethren to be "steadfast, unmovable, always abounding in the work of the Lord" (1 Cor 15:58); and indeed, if the case be otherwise, "the latter end is worse with them than the beginning" (2 Pet 2:20). But, if we are faithful to death, we shall receive a crown of life (Rev 2:10).

5. They that walk in Christ are progressive in their religion; they go forward in their journey Zion-ward. As the Apostle expresses it, they "grow in grace, and in the knowledge of our Lord and Saviour Jesus Christ" (2 Pet 3:18). Those that walk in Christ get more power both to do duties and subdue sins. They get more wisdom to serve God in every relation. In a word, they do not rest in any attainment, however great it may seem to be, for, by doleful experience, they have learned how deceitful their heart is and "therefore fear, lest a promise being left us of entering into rest, any ... come short of it" (Heb 4:1). Neither is their fear inactive, as in the wicked, but it proves effectual to make them press toward the mark of the prize of their high calling in Christ Jesus (Phil 3:14) and diligently to add to their faith virtue, and to virtue knowledge (2 Pet 1:5–8). This is walking in Christ! But if by your religion you don't grow wiser and better, but are like the door on the hinges which though it opens and shuts never moves out of the spot, going to duty and returning from it without getting more conformity to God, you have great reason to believe you never knew Christ and so never did walk as you are required in our text. But I proceed to the next general head, which is to show—

III. What the advantages of this way of walking are.

1. It is a plain way. It is so clearly chalked out that he who runs may read it. Our good God has so suited his directions to the meanest capacities that all such who once get into the way of wisdom, although they are weak, yea fools, yet they shall not err for want of instruction; "And an highway shall be there, and a way, and it shall be called the way of holiness; the unclean shall not pass over it; but it shall be for those, the wayfaring men, though fools, shall not err therein" (Isa 35:8). The way of sin is crooked (Ps 125:5);

but this way is straight and easy, "For my yoke is easy, and my burden is light" (Matt 11:30). Although the wisest are sometimes puzzled, it is not so much owing to the way or want of directions in it as to their not attending to or regarding the directions proposed in the divine word.

2. It is a comfortable way of walking. "Her ways are ways of pleasantness, and all her paths are peace" (Prov 3:17). Now there are several things which make it truly so—

a) They have the blessed Spirit, who is the Comforter, for their companion. "And I will pray the Father, and he shall give you another Comforter, that he may abide with you forever" (John 14:16). And can there be anything more comfortable than to be blessed with such an associate who enlightens the dark understandings, dissipates the distressing fears, and guides in all the difficulties they meet with in their way? Surely, no!

b) The holy Scriptures conduce to make walking in Christ comfortable. These things are written that your joy may be full (1 John 1:4). This is the end for which they were given, so God makes them to answer it completely. Oh, the unspeakable satisfaction that the gracious soul finds in them! For they are a light to his feet and a lamp to his path (Ps 119:105). They deter him from sin and excite him to duty. Yea, the good God oftentimes, by the promises as conduits, conveys soul refreshing cordials to his poor fainting people by which their withered and almost dead souls are refreshed as with new wine and quickened in their duty. Holy David said, "This is my comfort in my affliction: for thy word hath quickened me" (Ps 119:50). This makes God's word sweeter to the godly than honey and the honey comb and more to be desired than gold, yea than much fine gold (Ps 19:10), for they are the joy of the heart. "Thy words were found, and I did eat them; and thy word was unto me the joy and rejoicing of my heart" (Jer 15:16).

c) The holy ordinances make it exceeding comfortable to walk in Christ, this being the end for which they were instituted.

1) Prayer: what tongue can express the satisfaction which arises from the right performance of this duty? By it the true Christian is both honored and eased. The former, in that he who is but a worm, yes, less than a worm, is permitted to speak to the great and infinitely glorious God, and that at all times and in all places without exception; the latter, in that he speaks to one who he knows is both willing and able to help him for his ears are ever open to his people's cry (Ps 34:15). Is it not a comfort to be permitted to speak to the Beloved of your souls—to ask him for the supply of your wants and to complain to him of all your sorrows? This is the privilege of all real

Christians. They may come to their Father's throne with a filial freedom, with a holy, humble boldness (Heb 4:16). By this they are often so freed from their distresses that they are, with holy Hannah, no more sorrowful (1 Sam 1:18).

2) Praise: this, being the work of angels, cannot but be very comfortable to them, for in it they make a joyful noise to the God of their salvation (Ps 95:1). But this is better felt than expressed.

However, brethren, the time would fail me to speak of the comforts which arise from a right attendance upon all divine ordinances; how he pours out his Spirit in baptism, makes himself known in the breaking of bread at his holy supper, warms the heart by Christian fellowship, and inflames the affections by pious meditations, for while they muse, the fire burns (Ps 39:3). Neither have I time to speak of how useful the Sabbath is to those that fear God, as it unbends their minds from worldly pursuits, draws their hearts out to God, and fits them for the duties of the week following; not to mention the inward satisfactions they have from it, for indeed it is their delight (Isa 58:13). The Sabbath is doubtless rendered the more delightful by the ministers of the gospel, whose work it is therein to preach deliverance to the captives and recovery of sight to the blind and to set at liberty them that are bruised (Luke 4:18); and also to say to those that are of a fearful heart, be strong (Isa 35:3–4). These things considered clearly prove that walking in Christ is comfortable beyond compare.

3. It is profitable way of walking.

a) They are freed from the soul-damning obligation to law with which they were bound so that there is an open defiance bid to charge them with a crime. "Who shall lay anything to the charge of God's elect, it is God that justifies," and seeing it is the Judge himself who justifies, who can condemn them? (Rom 8:33). None surely! So that though the wicked (as alas they do to their own hurt!) labor to blacken believer's characters by notorious untruths which they maliciously report of them and anathematize them as the most execrable of mankind, deserving to be driven from men, to dwell with Nebuchadnezzar among the beasts, yea, sentence them as those that shall dwell with devils and damned ghosts, yet God shall pronounce them just, to the confusion of their adversaries.

b) They have the profit of friendship with God. "Ye are my friends, if ye do whatsoever I command you" (John 15:14). This tie of friendship which is between God and believers is of the strongest possible nature. It is that of the Father with his children: "I will . . . be a Father to you, and ye shall be my sons and daughters, saith the Lord almighty" (2 Cor 6:18). It is that between the husband and the wife, "thy Maker is thy husband; the Lord of hosts is his name" (Isa 54:5). It is between brethren, "Go to my brethren, and say unto them, I ascend unto my Father and your Father, to my God and your God" (John 20:17). Now, is not this an infinite advantage to be related to God in such ways? Hereby we are enabled to address him with boldness for a supply of all our wants. Nothing is more reasonable than that children should go to their Father, who is able and willing to help them, and cast all their care upon him who cares for them (1 Pet 5:7). Again, surely it is very beneficial to be wedded to One who is responsible for their debt, for thereby they are freed from the demands of the law, it not being the wife's business to pay the debts. After the same manner, the Christian is free in Christ, and "if the Son therefore shall make you free, you shall be free indeed" (John 8:36). Now, who would not walk in Christ with such benefits as these?

c) They have peace. "Peace I leave with you, my peace I give unto you: not as the world giveth, give I unto you" (John 14:27).

1. Peace with God (Col 1:21).

2. Peace with their neighbor; for although believers are hated by others, yet they do whatever lies in them to live peaceably with all men (Rom 12:18).

3. Peace in their conscience, which is so comfortable that it causes those that have it to rejoice. "For our rejoicing is this, the testimony of our conscience, that in simplicity and godly sincerity, not with fleshly wisdom, but by the grace of God, we have had our conversation in the world" (2 Cor 1:12). As nothing is more tormenting and distracting than a guilty conscience, so on the other hand, nothing is more sweet and comfortable than peace of mind. "For if our hearts condemn us not, then have we confidence toward God" (1 John 3:21).

d) Such as walk in Christ are favored with the earnest of their inheritance. In Romans 8:18, the Apostle words it as "the glory which shall be revealed in us." "These things have I written unto you that believe on the name of the Son of God, that ye may know that ye have eternal life" (1 John 5:13). This is nothing else but Canaan's clusters or the first fruits of that glorious harvest which they are to reap eternally with the fullness of joy in God's presence, at whose "right hand are pleasures forevermore" (Ps 16:11). "To him that ordereth his conversation aright will I show the salvation of God" (Ps 50:23). In short, believers are favored with all things that are necessary

APPENDIX 2: ADDITIONAL GREAT AWAKENING SERMONS

for their comfort in body and soul, in life and at death, for time and eternity. Our blessed Lord said, "I am the bread of life: he that cometh to me shall never hunger; and he that believeth on me shall never thirst" (John 6:35). Now seeing that walking in Christ is so plain, comfortable, and beneficial a way of walking, then surely the Apostle exhorts us wisely, "As ye have received Christ Jesus the Lord, so walk ye in him." This much for the doctrinal part of the discourse; I therefore proceed to the improvement.

Improvement one: For information.

Is walking in Christ comfortable? Then this doctrine serves to refute the false notions of those who industriously labor to represent religion as a dull and melancholy business, only fit for those who have become unable to taste the pleasures of sense! Although those who do so represent it pretend themselves to be the wits of the age, yet they are really only fools. They would do better to discover their ignorance of true religion and their enmity against God and holiness than to listen to their own foolish speeches. For wisdom's ways are ways of pleasantness, and how such persons as are false witnesses against the way of truth shall escape the righteous judgments of God without a very speedy and thorough repentance, I know not! By their words, they reflect immediate dishonor upon Christ who is the way, the truth, and the life; and like the Pharisees of old, they neither enter into the kingdom themselves nor suffer other poor souls that would to enter.

It informs us that real comfort is only to be had in being truly and unfeignedly holy or religious, for as the Psalmist says, "in the keeping of God's commandments there is great reward" (Ps 19:11). But on the contrary, "Unto them that are contentious, and do not obey the truth, but obey unrighteousness, indignation, and wrath, tribulation and anguish upon every soul of man that doeth evil, of the Jew first, and also of the Gentile" (Rom 2:8–9).

Improvement two: For examination.

Determine whether or not you have received Christ according to the doctrinal description of it, that is, with understanding, sincerity, wholly, only, expecting salvation by none other but him. Try yourselves deliberately by these things. If you find you have not, as I believe is the sad case of many in this house, I must tell you that you have refused him for he has been fairly offered to you. So you are miserable, not only because you lack Christ Jesus the most excellent of all mercies that others enjoy, but because you have refused him, you are exposed to eternal damnation. "He that rejecteth me, and receiveth not my words, hath one that judgeth him: The word that I have spoken, the same shall judge him in the last day [or day of judgment]" (John 12:48). For "he that believeth not, [or receiveth not Christ, which are equivalent terms] is condemned already" (John 3:18). Yea, the wrath of God is already upon him (verse 36). That wrath, which will as surely be the death and damnation of your souls as his favor is their life and salvation, you have incurred by the breach of his laws and inflamed by rejecting the only remedy provided for perishing souls. This wrath is treasured up for you against the day of wrath and revelation of the righteous judgment of God (Rom 2:5).

But on the contrary, if there are any here, as I hope indeed there are, who have received the blessed Lord Jesus, you are told your duty in this precious text, "As ye have received Christ Jesus the Lord, so walk ye in him." In order that you may better do this I shall humbly propose for your consideration a few directions; which may the good God grant you hearts to observe and practice.

Direction one.

Labor after the exercise and increase of love to the Lord Jesus Christ. Love is so necessary that none can walk with Christ without it. "Can two walk together except they be agreed?" (Amos 3:3). This the Apostle knew well, and therefore he exhorts the Ephesians to "walk in love, as Christ also hath loved us, and hath given himself for us an offering and a sacrifice to God for a sweet-smelling savor" (Eph 5:2). If this grace is in you and abounds, it will make you abundant in doing and patient in suffering for Christ's sake. Thus it was with Jacob for his beloved Rachel (Gen 29:20). And much more so will it be with you if that holy fire is kindled and increased in your breasts. No labor, however hard it is, will you cease doing for him; no suffering will be accounted too painful, nor life itself dear to you, if you can but win him. When Christ is the soul's treasure, the heart is with him, and this necessarily produces a heavenly conversation which is the glory of every Christian, for it yields for him inexpressible comfort in his own mind. "The work of righteousness shall be peace; and the effect of righteousness quietness and assurance forever" (Isa 32:17).

APPENDIX 2: ADDITIONAL GREAT AWAKENING SERMONS

But on the other hand, if love is not exercised, then the worship of God will be wearisome to you so that your hearts will devise excuses to neglect or slightly perform it. Then sin will appear small so that you won't watch against it as formerly. Thus if mercy prevent not, you will fall to the scandal of your holy profession and the wounding of your own souls. In order to excite your love, it will be necessary to think frequently and seriously upon the personal and mediatorial excellencies of Christ, as well as his communicated goodness to you. Consider what he is in himself, what he has done and suffered for you, and what he has conferred upon you.

Direction two.

Keep a strict watch over your hearts.

1. The heart is notoriously deceitful and therefore must not be trusted by any wise man. It is the characteristic of a fool to do so. "He that trusteth in his own heart is a fool" (Prov 28:26). It often proves itself as a deceitful bow (Ps 78:57), which though it seems as if it would send the arrow to the mark, yet drops it at the foot of the archer. After this manner does the heart deceive by seeming sincerity, when in the meantime it is desperately wicked (Jer 17:9). To prevent this, you must be very watchful, lest you be cheated at last and so ruined thereby.

2. It ought to be watched because it is the fountain of action; out of it are the issues of death and the issues of life. The whole stream of our conversation will be determined by whether the heart is holy or impure, just as our blessed Lord said, "A good man out of the good treasure of his heart bringeth forth that which is good, and an evil man out of the evil treasure of his heart bringeth forth that which is evil, for of the abundance of the heart the mouth speaketh" (Luke 6:45); therefore "look to it, lest there be in any of you an evil heart of unbelief in departing from the living God" (Heb 3:12).

Direction three.

Shun all sin, yea, the very appearance of evil (1 Thess 5:22). As all sin in general is faithfully and carefully to be shunned without exception, so these sins particularly:

1. Undue thoughts of God and religion; either that he is severe in afflicting you or unmindful of your afflicted condition. Never suffer yourselves

to think that the kind God is not an austere master, reaping where he has not sown, or that he will suffer the impenitent sinner to pass unpunished, however secretly he may hide his wickedness. By these and similar ways of conceiving of God, he is grievously wronged. Beware also of thinking or speaking of religion as a melancholy business, admitting of no comfort or pleasure, or that in the practice of it you shall meet with no trouble. If you represent it in any of these colors, you wrong it, for there is real pleasure in it (Prov 3:17) just as also upon the heavenly road, you shall pass through tribulations and those not a few (Acts 14:22).

2. Carefully guard against unbelief both of the promises and of the threatenings of God. Unbelief is very detrimental to walking with Christ. Belief in the threatenings of God deters from sin. Belief in the promises of God excites to duty. If we could believe that walking in Christ is as comfortable as it is represented to be by the promises of the gospel and that departing from the living God a thing of such evil and bitterness as it is declared to be by the threatenings of the law, surely we would be more careful how we walked. But if neither is believed, and both are disregarded, then such unbelief will ruin the poor sinner. Therefore, unbelief must be shunned as a most destructive and soul-damning evil.

3. Labor to keep your heart from loving the world or the things of the world, for "If any man love the world, the love of the Father is not in him" (1 John 2:15). This sin has ruined many fair professors; it caused Demas to turn aside from his profession, "Demas hath forsaken me, having loved this present world" (2 Tim 4:10). This made Judas sell his master and Lord. Yes, and if it gets possession of your hearts, it will cause you to do both; therefore, shun it.

4. Shun all manner of uncleanness in heart, speech, and action as that which is inconsistent with and destructive of walking in Christ. "Be not deceived, neither fornicators, nor idolaters, nor adulterers, nor effeminate, nor abusers of themselves with mankind . . . shall inherit the kingdom of God" (1 Cor 6:9–10). Therefore, "Dearly beloved, I beseech you as strangers and pilgrims, abstain from fleshly lusts, which war against the soul" (1 Pet 2:11). Say to the first motions of it, as did a holy, though sorely tempted Joseph, "How then can I do this great wickedness, and sin against God?" (Gen 39:9). Yea, let it not be once named among you, as becometh saints.

5. Shun cowardice in the cause of God, for it is a dishonor to him. Such a sin must not be allowed even in the most trying times. This evil we are guilty of when we cease to do those duties he has required of us for fear of

abuse by those we live among. God lacks neither power nor goodness to protect us in his service, and even to imply that he does is blasphemy of the highest degree. And as it is dishonoring to God, so also it is destructive in those in whom it prevails. "But the fearful and unbelieving... shall have their part in the lake which burneth with fire and brimstone" (Rev 21:8).

6. Shun confidence in your own power or goodness. This is fatal to the soul. By it you will be kept from former dependence upon God, who alone is your stay and support. To deter you from this, remember Peter, who, although he thought he could die for Christ, was beat off from following him by the breath of a servant girl.

Direction four.

Study to know the Scriptures. Search these holy oracles and treasure them up plentifully in your memories, that you may by them be able to repel your adversaries as with a sword.

Direction five.

Be often at the throne of grace. Pray without ceasing, for the Lord desires you to enquire of him concerning all the things you need. Take care that you pray with humility, faith, and fervor, otherwise you need not think of praying.

But to conclude, dear brethren! I need not tell you that the eyes of men and angels are upon us, for we are, according to the Apostle, a gazing-stock to angels and to men. Some are watching that they may find something whereby they may reproach us and the way of truth professed by us. Others are watching that they may learn by our example to walk in Christ. In both cases, a fall will be very hurtful to the observers, to say nothing of the hurt we shall do thereby to our own souls and the dishonor to God to whom we are bound by the most solemn covenant-obligation to glorify. Therefore, let us watch and be sober, walking as children of the day, for our enemy goes about like a roaring lion seeking whom he may devour.

In order that you may be delivered from this loathsome enemy, "Let the God of peace, that brought again from the dead our Lord Jesus Christ, that great shepherd of the sheep, through the blood of the everlasting covenant, make you perfect in every good work to do his will, working in you that which is well pleasing in his sight, through Jesus Christ; to whom be glory for ever and ever. Amen."

APPENDIX 3

Society Rules and Orders

Appendix 3a: *Orders and Expectations for Society Members*[1]

1. To be just in all their dealings, even to an exemplary strictness: as Matt 5:16, 20; Matt 7:12.

2. To pray many times every day, remembering our continual dependence upon God, both for spiritual and temporal things. 1 Thess 5:17.

3. To partake of the Lord's Supper at least once a month, if not prevented by a reasonable impediment. 1 Cor 11:26; Luke 22:19.

4. To practice the profoundest meekness and humility. Matt 11:29.

5. To watch against censuring others. Matt 7:1.

6. To accustom themselves to holy thoughts in all places. Ps 2–3.

7. To be helpful one to another. 1 Cor 12:26.

8. To exercise tenderness, patience, and compassion, towards all men. Titus 3:2.

9. To make reflections on themselves when they read the Holy Bible, or other good books, and when they hear sermons. 1 Cor 10:11.

10. To shun all foreseen occasions of evil; as evil company, known temptations, &c. 1 Thess 5:22.

11. To think often on the different estates of the glorified and the damned, in the unchangeable eternity, to which we are hastening. Luke 16:25.

12. To examine themselves every night, what good or evil they have done in the day past. 2 Cor 13:5.

---

1. Heitzenrater, *Mirror and Memory*, 38.

13. To keep a private fast once a month, (especially near their approach to the Lord's Table) if at their own disposal; or to fast from some meal when they may conveniently. Matt 6:16; Luke 5:35
14. To mortify the flesh with its affections, and lust. Gal 5:19, 24.
15. To advance in heavenly-mindedness, and in all grace. 1 Pet 3:8.
16. To shun spiritual pride, and the effects of it; as railing, anger, peevishness, and impatience of contradiction, &c.
17. To pray for the whole Society in their private prayers. James 5:16.
18. To read pious books often for their edification.
19. To be continually mindful of the great obligation of this special profession of religion, and to walk so circumspectly, that none may be offended or discouraged from it by what they see in them, nor occasion be given to any, to speak reproachfully of it.
20. To shun all manner of affectation and moroseness, and to be of a civil and obliging deportment to all men.

APPENDIX 3: SOCIETY RULES AND ORDERS

Appendix 3b: *The Nature, Design, and General Rules of the United Societies*[2]

1. In the latter end of the year 1739, eight or ten persons came to me in London, who appeared to be deeply convinced of sin, and earnestly groaning for redemption. They desired (as did two or three more the next day) that I would spend some time with them in prayer, and advise them how to flee from the wrath to come; which they saw continually hanging over their heads. That we might have more time for this great work, I appointed a day when they might all come together, which from thenceforward they did every week, namely, on Thursday, in the evening. To these, and as many more as desired to join with them, (for their number increased daily), I gave those advices, from time to time, which I judged most needful for them; and we always concluded our meeting with prayer suited to their several necessities.

2. This was the rise of the United Society, first in London, and then in other places. Such a society is no other than "a company of men having the form and seeking the power of godliness, united in order to pray together, to receive the word of exhortation, and to watch over one another in love, that they may help each other to work out their salvation."

3. That it may the more easily be discerned, whether they are indeed working out their own salvation, each society is divided into smaller companies, called *classes*, according to their respective places of abode. There are about twelve persons in every class; one whom is styled *the Leader*. It is his business, (1.) To see each person in his class once a week at least, in order to inquire how their souls prosper; to advise, reprove, comfort, or exhort, as occasion may require; to receive what they are willing to give toward the relief of the poor. (2.) To meet the Minister and the Stewards of the society once a week, in order to inform the Minister of any that are sick, or of any that walk disorderly, and will not be reproved; to pay to the Stewards what they have received of their several classes in the week preceding; and to show their account of what each person has contributed.

4. There is only one condition previously required in those who desire admission into these societies, —a desire "to flee from the wrath to come, to be saved from their sins." But wherever this is really fixed in the soul, it will be shown by its fruits. It is therefore expected of all who continue therein, that they should continue to evidence their desire of salvation:

---

2. Wesley, *The Works of John Wesley*, 8:269-71.

APPENDIX 3: SOCIETY RULES AND ORDERS

First, by doing no harm, by avoiding evil in every kind; especially that which is most practiced—Such is, the taking the name of God in vain, the profaning the day of the Lord, either by doing ordinary work thereon, or by buying or selling; drunkenness, buying or selling spirituous liquors, or drinking them, unless in cases of extreme necessity; fighting, quarreling, brawling; brother going to law with brother; returning evil for evil, or railing for railing; the using many words in buying or selling; they buying and selling uncustomed goods; the giving or taking things usury, that is unlawful interest; uncharitable or unprofitable conversation, particularly speaking evil of Magistrates or of Ministers; doing what we know is not for the glory of God, as the "putting of gold or costly apparel"; the taking such diversions as cannot be used in the name of the Lord Jesus; the singing those songs, or reading those books, which do not tend to the knowledge or love of God; softness, and needing self-indulgence; laying up treasures upon the earth; borrowing without a probability of paying, or taking up goods without a probability of paying for them.

5. It is expected of all who continue in these societies, that they should continue to evidence their desire of salvation:

Secondly, by doing good, by being, in every kind, merciful after their power, as they have opportunity, doing good of every possible sort, and as far as is possible, to all men;—to their bodies, of the ability which God giveth, by giving food to the hungry, by clothing the naked, by visiting or helping them that are sick, or in prison;—to their souls, by instructing, reproving, or exhorting all they have any intercourse with; trampling under foot that enthusiastic doctrine of devils, that "we are not to do good unless our heart be free to do it." By doing good especially to them that are the household of faith, or groaning so to be; employing them preferably to others, buying one of another, helping each other in business, and so much the more, because the world will love its own, and them only. By all possible diligence and frugality, that the gospel be not blamed. By running with patience the race that is set before them, "denying themselves, and taking up their cross daily"; submitting to bear the reproach of Christ, to be as the filth and offscouring of the world; and looking men should "say all manner of evil of them falsely for the Lord's sake."

6. It is expected of all who desire to continue in these societies, that they should continue to evidence their desire of salvation:

Thirdly, by attending upon all the ordinances of God. Such are, the public worship of God, the ministry of the word, either read or expounded, the supper of the Lord, family and private prayer, searching the Scriptures, and fasting, or abstinence.

7. These are the General Rules of our societies; all of which we are taught of God to observe, even in his written word, the only rule, and the sufficient rule, both of our faith and practice. And all these, we know, his Spirit writes on every truly awakened heart. If there be any among us who observe them not, who habitually break any of them, let it be made known unto them who watch over their soul as they that must give an account. We will admonish him of the error of his ways; we will bear with him for a season. But then if he repent not, he hath no more place among us. We have delivered our own souls.

John Wesley
Charles Wesley

Bibliography

Balleine, G.R. *A History of the Evangelical Party*. London: Longmans, Green, and Company, 1911.
Bready, J. Wesley. *England: Before and After Wesley*. New York: Russel & Russel, 1971.
Cairns, Earle E. *An Endless Line of Splendor*. Wheaton, IL: Tyndale House, 1986.
Durnbaugh, Donald F. *European Origins of the Brethren*. Elgin, IL: The Brethren Press, 1958.
Edwards, Jonathan. *Jonathan Edwards on Revival: A Narrative of Surprising Conversions*. Carlisle, PA: The Banner of Truth Trust, 1994.
Fish, Henry C. *Handbook of Revivals*. Harrisonburg, VA: Gano Books, 1988.
Fitchett, W.H. *Wesley and His Century, A Study of Spiritual Forces*. Cincinnati, OH: Jennings and Graham, 1908.
George, M.D. *London Life in the Eighteenth Century*. New York: Harper and Row, 1964.
Gillis, John. *Historical Collections of Accounts of Revival*. Carlisle, PA: Banner of Truth Trust, 1981.
Gleason, Michael F. *When God Walked on Campus: A Brief History of Evangelical Awakenings at American Colleges and Universities*. Ontario, Canada: Joshua Press, 2002, 2013.
Goldsmith, Oliver. *Citizen of the World*. London: J.M. Dent and Company, 1891.
Green, J.R. *History of the English People, Vol. 3*. New York: Harper & Brothers, 1900.
———. *Short History of the English People*. New York: American Book Company, 1916.
Heitzenrater, Richard P. *Mirror and Memory*. Nashville, TN: Kingswood Books, 1989.
———. *Wesley and the People Called Methodists*. Nashville, TN: Abingdon, 1995.
Lecky, W.H. *A History of England in the Eighteenth Century*, Vol. 1. New York: D. Appleton and Company, 1892.
Lescelius, Robert H. "The Great Awakening: A Pattern Revival." *Reformation and Revival*, Vol. 4, No. 3, Summer 1995.
Lewis, A.J. *Zinzendorf: The Ecumenical Pioneer*. Philadelphia, PA: Westminster, 1962.
Macfarlan, D. *The Revivals of the Eighteenth Century, Particularly at Cambuslang*. Wheaton, IL: Richard Owen Roberts, 1980.
Maxson, Charles Hartshorn. *The Great Awakening in the Middle Colonies*. Gloucester, MA: Peter Smith, 1958.
Meeks, Wayne A. *The First Urban Christians*. New Haven: Yale University Press, 1983.
Moorman, John R.H. *A History of the Church in England*. New York: Morehouse-Barlow Company, 1967.

BIBLIOGRAPHY

Poole-Connor, E.J. *Evangelism in England*. London: The Fellowship of Independent Evangelical Churches, 1951.

Roberts, Richard Owen, ed. *Salvation in Full Color*. Wheaton, IL: International Awakening, 1994.

———. *Whitefield in Print*. Wheaton, IL: Richard Owen Roberts, 1988.

Smith, Lisa. *The First Great Awaking in Colonial American Newspapers: A Shifting Story*, Plymouth, UK: Lexington Books, 2012.

Smollett, T. *The History of England*, Vol. 1. Philadelphia, PA: S. Parker Printers, 1828.

Stoeffler, F. Ernest, ed. *Continental Pietism and the Early American Christianity*. Grand Rapids, MI: Eerdmans, 1976.

Sweet, William Warren. *The Story of Religion in America*. New York: Harper Brothers, 1939.

Tracy, Joseph. *The Great Awakening*. Oxford: The Banner of Truth Trust, 1976.

Trevelyan, G.M. *Illustrated English Social History*, Vol. 3. New York: David McKay Company Inc., 1942.

Tuberville, A.S. *Johnson's England*. Oxford: Clarendon, 1933.

Tyerman, Luke. *The Life of the Reverend George Whitefield, two volumes*, Azel, TX: Need of the Times Publishers, 1995.

———. *The Life of the Reverend John Wesley*, Vol. 1. New York: Harper and Brothers, 1872.

Watson, David Lowes. *The Early Methodists Class Meeting*. Nashville, TN: Discipleship Resources, 1985.

Wesley, John. *The Journal of John Wesley*, 8 Volumes. Edited by Nehemiah Curnock. London: Epworth, 1938.

———. *The Letters of the Rev. John Wesley*, 8 Volumes. Edited by John Telford. London: Epworth, 1931.

———. *The Works of John Wesley*, 13 Volumes. London: Wesleyan Conference, 1872, reprinted ed. Grand Rapids. MI: Zondervan Press, 1958.

Whitefield, George. *George Whitefield's Journals*. Carlisle, PA: Banner of Truth Trust, 1992.

Wood, A. Skevington. *The Burning Heart*. Minneapolis, MN: Bethany House, 1978.

———. *The Inextinguishable Blaze*. Grand Rapid, MI: Eerdmans, 1960.

www.ingramcontent.com/pod-product-compliance
Lightning Source LLC
Chambersburg PA
CBHW072143160426
43197CB00012B/2230